The Memoir of an Incarcerated Heart

By: Bishelya Hooper

ISBN-13: 978-0615793047

ISBN-10: 0615793045

This book is dedicated to all the spouses, significant others, children, and family members of those who are incarcerated. May you take refuge and solstice in your faith and draw the strength to endure and understand your situation. It is my hope that you will gain inspiration and motivation from my story.

Acknowledgements

To my husband, Willie: your love, devotion, and unwavering support have shown me fresher insight and renewed meaning to life. I thank you for inspiring and encouraging me to share my experiences through this memoir. I appreciate your perspective, opinions, and point of view. I am grateful that you have been so comfortable with allowing me to write about some of the intimate details of our marriage. You have been completely amazing and understanding through this entire process. I love you more than my heart can say.

To my children, my fantastic four: I thank you all for being so helpful, for keeping quiet, and helping around the house. You all have proven that you can be so cooperative and understanding, especially when it is needed. I know that I have been a little preoccupied at times but it is only because I wanted this to be great. I appreciate everything and all that you have done to help me. I love you guys more than life itself.

To the rest of my family, friends, associates, and well-wishers: I thank you all for all your guidance, prayers, friendship, and support. While there are too many of you to name individually, just know that each of you are etched in my heart. Hugs, Love, & Blessings!

Introduction

Understanding the Basics

In order to prepare to write a memoir that is so personal to me, it was important that I conducted research and immersed myself with accurate facts. These facts are meant to shed light on the magnitude of people, who like myself, are affected by the growing population of incarcerated individuals in the United States. I warn you that the facts are astounding, yet serve to put the subject into perspective for those who truly do not understand or even know how severe the problem is. Even with the statistics, people seem to not fully understand the true complexity of the problem until they have been affected by the situation in a more intimate, more personal way. I'm not implying that others don't understand it's just that when you are closely related to a situation, the points hit a little harder.

According to various prison studies and statistical analysis, America has the highest number of inmates in the world. Although America only represents just 5 percent of the world's population, we are housing the largest number of inmates, which is about 25 percent. As of today, there are roughly 2.2 million people incarcerated in the United States, which equates to roughly 1 out of 142 people. Although men account for 94 percent of the prison population, the fastest growing prison population is women. It is believed that the reason for the high number of incarcerated people is because of the new sentencing guidelines that have been set forth not only by the government but by each of the individual states. The passage of new mandatory sentence minimums, 3 strikes laws, habitual offender laws, career criminal laws, truth-in sentencing laws, abolishment of parole, and disproportionate sentencing are responsible for the large number of incarcerated people. Lawmakers created these laws with the intent to deter criminal activity, relieve taxpayers of financial responsibility, and reduce recidivism. However, the opposite happened. These laws have attributed more to the staggering, growing number of incarcerated people. These laws have created longer sentences, some being disproportionate in relation to the offense. Prison populations have increased at an astounding rate, resulting in mass incarceration.

When the subject of an incarcerated person comes about, you will often find that the first thing that people want to know is why, how, and when did a crime take place. These questions take place first and foremost without much consideration of the offender, their background, and their families. The crime itself takes precedence above any and everything. In all honesty, this is very understandable. I am sure that no victim of a heinous crime is concerned with the family of the person that hurt them. They do not care about the offender's loved ones who sit on the other side of the table or the fact that they too are also affected by that action. I completely understand. We all believe in fairness and justice and that people should be held accountable for their actions. Because of that, the focus is put on justice being served and making a person accountable for their actions. There is rarely mention or even a thought as to an offender's families, except for in the process of establishing a motive, social histories, or understanding a reason for the person to have committed a crime. Justice is what is being sought, and rightfully so. However, we can't just close our eyes to the lives on the other side.

Now, while there is no set profile for a person that has committed a crime, I have found that majority of prisoners come from the working class and the poorest sections of society. These individuals may lack in education and vocational skills needed to seek and obtain employment opportunities. This barrier of unemployment leads directly to financial instability. There is also the lack familiar support. Many come from single parent homes or were being raised by other family members such as older siblings, grandmothers, and aunts. Lastly, there is the lack residential stability. Moving from neighborhood to neighborhood or living in unusual conditions such as in hotels, shelters, or subsidized housing brings about a level of entrapment and despair. These barriers are the culprits that have contributed to the irresponsible behaviors of offenders. The sad fact, is that majority of these individuals are African American males. The rate of incarceration of African Americans is alarming.

African Americans tend to receive sentences that are harsher, more severe, and with longer confinement in comparison to their counterparts of other races and ethnicities. Racial profiling, shady lawmaking officials, and the profit revenue that is generated from the operation of private prisons and their practices have also attributed to the mass incarceration of so many individuals. The private prison industry has profited greatly from the revenue that is generated from the incarceration of individuals. More money is spent on the construction of prisons than on the building colleges and the creation of vocational training or other educational programs. These tools are needed to help others obtain sustainable employment and to deter them from the criminal activities that for many, seem to be the answer to life's problems.

I believe that education is the key to success. When time, money, and energy are invested into education, individuals and the world as a whole reaps its benefits. Obtaining an education creates the opportunity for advancement in economic status, confidence, and self-esteem, which in turn makes living life as a law abiding, productive citizen the more desirable way to live. Circumstances sometimes create tension and lead to disparity which seems to be one of the reasons that a person is even driven to commit a crime. I am not saying that is an excuse but it is definitely a reason. If equal opportunities for education and employment are made, I honestly believe that the crime rate will drop. To me, these statistics shed light onto the backgrounds and perhaps offers some kind of explanations as to the reasons that some crimes even take place. In order for you to find a solution to a problem, you must identify it and map out the reasons as to why the problem even exists. It is only then that you will be able to strategize and find a solution.

During my research, I have yet to find any statistics that show that mass incarceration has proven to be effective in the prevention and determent of crime. In fact, I have encountered just the opposite. Unsanitary living conditions, inadequate healthcare, corruption, and the *greed of corporate and government officials have made an extreme impact in the arena of mass incarceration. Combined with understaffing, correctional officer misconduct, and the lack of adequate educational and vocational training, all these things have created a system that breeds of extreme violence and desolation. This in turn undermines the concept of correction and rehabilitation. Violence and tensions inside of prisons have escalated, making prison seem more like an active war zone rather than a place of rehabilitation. Prisoners often find themselves in situations of having to argue for the mere basic necessities such as nutritional food and adequate health care. I have noticed that the number of those incarcerated has risen and that there are even state prison departments that have a "waiting list" of people that are currently being housed in local jails who are waiting to be transferred to state prisons. Mass incarceration has served no real purpose other than to create an environment that makes preparation for a successful return to society a long, difficult, and tedious one.*

Please understand that I in no way condone or support criminal behavior. I understand that some people commit crimes out of sheer cruelty and evilness rather than for necessity. There are no excuses for those things or even crime period. But we must understand that there are many people who have committed crimes out of necessity or pure desperation. Some are clearly victims themselves to the unjust and unfair pressures and circumstances of life. To understand and to reduce recidivism, we must explore the very things that seem to make criminal activity more feasible in contrast to obeying and respecting laws. And until society addresses the issues that contribute to the commission of crimes, the problem will continue to persist and the prison population will continue to increase.

After reviewing the statistics, it is discouraging and even alarming as to the number of individuals that are incarcerated. With all the studies and statistics that I have read, I have yet to have read a comprehensive, detailed study that reflects on the number of spouses, children, and other family members that are affected by the incarceration of their loved ones. Incarceration does not only affect the offender but their families. One out of 43 children has a parent that is incarcerated. This statistic accounts for the large number of children that are often left without a parent and in some cases without a parent at all. Elderly grandparents and other family members are forced to raise children who would otherwise be put into state custody themselves and forced to unwittingly suffer the same fate as their parents. Incarceration of loved ones' leaves homes and families broken. It creates a cycle of repetition as the family unit is displaced and in some cases even destroyed. Questions are left unanswered. Emotional scars fill their minds, hearts, and spirits. Lives are immensely affected.

The families of the incarcerated are the forgotten population who love, respect, and cherish their incarcerated loved one despite their criminal convictions. They are often overshadowed by the criminal arrests, court hearings, and convictions. More of the focus in set on the individual who committed the act and to whom the act was committed upon rather than the families that are affected and left behind. It is often that the families of the

*incarcerated are left in the dark, uninformed, and even
ridiculed because of the unconditional love of their
incarcerated loved one and for their choice to support them
despite of their convictions. They are subjected to
judgement, torment, and disrespect because of the actions
of their loved ones. The families' voices are lost, their hearts
ache, and their eyes are filled with tears. They are left to
pick up the pieces of their lives and move on in the best
possible way that they can. This proves to sometimes be a
difficult but necessary task.*

*While there is the understanding that a person must
pay for their mistakes, let us open our eyes and not forget
that despite their flaws, those who are incarcerated are
loved by many. Their families have the right to do just that.
They are sentenced to time away from the people that they
love and who love them. They are locked down in the
painful tragedy of criminal misfortune. Not only does
incarceration affect the incarcerated loved one but it
affects those that care about them and love them
unconditionally.*

*It is easy to sympathize with crime victims and
rightfully so. We must never forget that victims deserve
compassion and justice. We must also understand that
there are consequences to our actions and the choices that
we make. We must accept personal responsibility for the
things that we have done and show remorse to those whom
we have hurt. Although we understand and have sympathy
for victims and their situations, let us not forget those other
innocent people who are affected as well, the families of the
incarcerated. May their voices be heard, may their hearts
be healed, and may they find the peace, solstice, and*

strength to endure the eventful and unpredictable journey that incarceration brings.

When I first married my husband, I started to hear people refer to me as a "prison wife". Personally, I do not wish to identify with that term. I feel that the term negates a stigma of degradation and humiliation. People often say that term to mean the wife of a prisoner but the true definition actually reflects the opposite of that. Per several sources that I researched, a "prison wife" is defined as "an inmate who befriends a fellow prisoner, performing the duties normally expected of a real wife, and yes including sex, in exchange for protection and companionship". So, no, I do not identify with the term "prison wife". However, I am legally married to my husband. I am his wife. His current location does not define my position as his wife. I am his wife, pure and simply. And that is how I choose to be characterized and identified.

Although I am married to my husband, the love and loyalty to those that are incarcerated is not just reserved lawfully wedded wives. I respect and appreciate fiancé's, boyfriends, girlfriends, life partners, and significant others. There are many people who have put a lot of love, time, and life into their incarcerated loved ones and I do not want to diminish their importance or relevance because something as simple as legalities. Titled or not, we love our loved ones just as much as anyone could love someone else and with the same level of devotion, loyalty, and passion. We all go through so many things within our relationships and within society. We are all fighting a battle. We are often judged, ridiculed, and criticized for our choice to love those that society views as ruthless animals that are incapable of rehabilitation and who should be discarded and left to wither away.

As the wife of an incarcerated husband, I am constantly on a roller coaster ride of emotion. I am often pulled between the views of society and the feelings that I have for my husband. I do understand that there is the concept of "right and wrong" and that everyone has to be held accountable for their mistakes, no matter the circumstances. However, the greatest, purest emotion is love. The unconditional love that I have for him allows me to see him for who he truly is. It prevails regardless to the things that he has done to land himself in prison. It is that love that makes me fight harder and empathize with others. My love, loyalty, and devotion to him supersede any negative and jaded opinion that another may have. I see him as an individual, an imperfect man whose love and devotion mirrors that of my very own. I see a man of integrity who is making atonement for the wrongs of his past and the mistakes that he has made. I see a man whose vision is clairvoyant and affixed on being a better version of his prior self. I see a man of divine strength and with a renewed purpose who will return to society and follow the path of greatness to which he has been blessed with. And I will take this journey with him.

The path that we have been ordained to walk is our own to follow and yet we have chosen to travel that path in our marital unity, conquering every problem, celebrating every success together. There are many who share this same sentiment with their loved ones. I come from the same place; I know how it all feels. It is my hope that my true-life story will give a voice to those who are unheard or misunderstood. It is my hope that you gain something from my story. It is in this memoir where I will challenge you to take a deep look and understand what it is like inside, The Incarcerated Heart.

Chapter 1

How We Came To Be

    My relationship with my husband started about three years ago. I met him through another mutual acquaintance of ours. During that period of time, we were just friends. We had adopted the type of relationship were we felt like we could talk to one another about anything and everything. We created a bond that was built on loyalty, honesty, and love. We would share so much with each other. Nothing was off limits. Everything; the good, the bad, the ugly, and the indifferent was all on the table. I got to know him in a way that was not fueled by a need, desire, or want to be involved with him romantically but to bond with him more in an intellectual or spiritual way.

    He was my best friend. We laughed, joked, shared secrets, and all. I could talk to him about all my joys, hurt, and sorrows. He knew my passions, my desires, and my spirit. It was his words of encouragement and his gentle critiques that got me through a lot of tough times. He was that peace, comfort, and voice of reason. He had that male point of view that helped me to catch and notice things that I would have otherwise missed. It was his way of making things so much less complicated that made him so easy to talk to and confide in. I could share my inner thoughts, my deepest feelings, and my insatiable desires with him without the fear of being judged or misunderstood. Surely, he could do the same with me. For a man who was incarcerated, his ability to have someone to talk to on that level is rare but it is definitely desired. So, when the opportunity presented itself to have that type of relationship with someone that you could truly be yourself with, it was definitely something worth every effort.

Never at that time would I have imagined that we would become more than just friends. He was settled in his life with the things that he was doing and I was in a relationship with someone else. We were both happy and content with the things that we had going on outside of our friendship. During this time, our talks were frequent and lasted sometimes for hours. I would find myself falling asleep to the tone of his voice. It was just something about that deep yet gentle southern accent that would just soothe me to sleep. His southern slang was so saturated that there were times when I had to sit and closely pay attention to what he said. His damn accent was so thick that it seemed as if he was speaking a foreign language. Even now, I often reminisce on the days when I would sit on the side of the bed still and quiet so that I could concentrate on his words and quickly formulate a response. He is just as country as corn! But I just loved each and every minute of it.

So much time had passed and we still talked and communicated. Although we didn't talk every day, when we did, it was always for such a long period of time and we would just pick up like there was never even a pause. I would drop him an occasional note or send a card and some pictures just to let him know that he was thought of and that no matter what, we would always be friends. To say that I was not attracted to him would be false, I mean he is an incredibly attractive man but I made sure to never cross that line because I was in a relationship with someone else. But to say that there wasn't a little bit of curiosity about him in a more lustful way would undoubtedly be far from the truth. I mean, when you spend as much time conversing and connecting with someone on a more intellectual level, there is bound to be some kind of attraction. The fact that he was equally physically attractive was a plus too. Yes, it could be a platonic attraction but never the less, an attraction.

Due to circumstances beyond my control, I lost contact with my friend. Not a day went by that I did not think of him and wonder how he was doing. I sent messages and notes but for some reason, he was not returning any response. So I ended up wondering what I had did or what I had said for him to not respond. I hated the fact that I had not been in contact with my friend. I eventually found out the reason why, but he only admitted it to me later. Of course I will get to that a little while. But months had passed since I had spoken to my friend. I honestly and truly missed him. I missed his jokes, his laughter, and the way he used to say my name. I had been going through some things and I needed his listening ear and incredible advice. I just wanted my friend. Just when I thought that I had lost contact with my friend forever, the most awesome thing happened.

My sister and I decided to go for one of our annual road trips. It was just a time for us to get away from all the foolishness, take a break from the kids, and just enjoy hanging out and admiring the scenery. Since it was beginning to get cold, we wanted to take our trip before the bad weather would make it impossible for us to enjoy. We live in Virginia and it tends to get cold here very quickly, so *our only fair chance for some warm weather was to head down to the South. We went down there, relaxed, did some shopping, ate, drank, and just had the time of our lives. But the strange thing that was even in the midst of all of that, I still could not shake the fact that I was really missing my friend. I was so close to him yet still so far. So, after a weekend of us having a ball, we headed back home to Virginia. We were still in South Carolina when I told her to see if she knew someone that knew how to get in contact with Zulu. You have no idea how much I was praying for this miracle. My sister is a beast with the phone and the internet so I already knew that she was going to come back with some good news for me. She made a few calls to see who she could locate that knew Zulu. The only thing that was left to do was wait and see. We were riding, laughing, singing and reminiscing on our trip. Out of nowhere, guess what happened? Her damn phone had begun to ring. The number was unfamiliar so she was like "Shelle, cut the music. We got to see who this is". I was quiet as a church mouse, even my heart had felt like it had stopped beating. When I heard the voice on the other end of that phone say "What's Up", I knew it was him. They found my Zulu! I was extra hype. Part of me didn't know whether I wanted to cuss him out for not keeping in touch or just get all mushy. On the inside my organs was having a whole party but of course my cool ass wasn't about to act on the outside like I was feeling in the inside. I had to stay smooth and collected. I mean, that is what pretty women do, right? I was just so glad that I had pulled off the highway though. My toes were trembling!*

My sister passed me the phone and I don't know why it felt like my hand was shaking like a leaf. But like I said, I was too cool to not be collected. So I started off with an "Oh, you act like you can't call nobody?" He started to laugh, in that same country voice, and said "Nah, that ain't it. I ain't been in contact with nobody. I haven't had any way to get out to anyone". That gave me some relief. So, I filled him in on a few things. The main thing was that my ex and I were no longer together. Since he was always the one who gave me such good advice about it, I just really needed to hear his thoughts about that. He didn't say much, which was a little puzzling to me. He got real silent for a minute and then said to me "Well, you know one man's trash is another man's treasure". I was dumbfounded for a quick minute because I was expecting him to ask a bunch of questions about why or how we broke up. But somehow I could just sense that he had more to say but that he just didn't have the time. I mean we have been known to carry on a conversation for hours. But after a few more minutes of small talk, he said to me "I am going to call you later on, we need to catch up. What time will you be home?" I told him that I would be home at about midnight and that I could not wait for him to call. Dang, I just couldn't wait to talk to him.

We were still on the highway with 2 hours left to go when my phone began to light up. My sister was sound asleep, leaving me all alone with nothing but my music and my thoughts. But it didn't bother me because it is just something about driving that makes me so relaxed. I look down at my phone and there was a message that said "Drive safely. I can't wait to talk to you". My face just lit up.

19

I could not help but to recall the conversation that we had earlier. His tone and demeanor was so different. He was up to something and I was determined to find out what it was. I could not wait to get home. So, I turned up the music, bumped up the cruise control, and coasted back Virginia.

I arrived home at about 12:03 a.m. I didn't even unpack. I went to check on my sons, looked at the mail, and headed upstairs to my bedroom. I was in my bedroom for about 5 minutes when my phone rung. It was Zulu. I was so ready to fill him in on everything that had went on and then to see how he was doing. I had so much to get off my chest. The first thing I had planned to do was cuss him out in detail because he hadn't called and I was worried about him. Then I was going to fill him in with the update on the kids, my business plans, and my breakup. Here it is, I am getting myself all ready for the conversation with my "friend" and then all of a sudden I could feel that his tone in our conversation was beginning to change. He was just eerily quiet and that worried me. It was like he had something on his mind that he just wasn't saying. So, when I asked him why he didn't try to contact me in these past months, he started off with "Check this out". I just knew something major was about to come out of his mouth because any time he said that, that was always the case. I was anxious to hear what he about to say. I prepared and braced myself for what was about to come.

So, he continues with "Look, I had to back away from you for a minute". Suddenly, my mind had begun to race wondering what I had said or did to make him feel like that. I was speechless. I had felt like someone had punched me right in the stomach. After a few seconds, I mustered up what little strength I had left to ask "Why". He says "because I found myself falling for you. You were writing and sending me pictures, we were talking all the time and I just started falling for you. I was seeing you in a way that was more than a friendship. You were with someone else and I had to respect that but yeah, I started falling for you". Now for someone like me, who always had something to say, I went completely mute. You know the saying "the cat got your tongue"? The cat had got my tongue and ran down the damn street with it. I couldn't say anything. He nervously called my name and said "Damn, I messed up, didn't I?" I told him no, that I was glad that he told me, and that he should never feel like he had to keep anything from me. Well, at least now I knew why his ass wasn't calling me. That explained it. So needless to say, I didn't cuss him out like I had planned.

    Minutes passed by and we were doing the small talk thing again and that is when he said "So what are you going to do with that piece of information that I gave you earlier? Are we going to try this relationship thing or do you just want to remain friends? I want more but, do you?" It felt like my heart was doing the two-step inside of my chest. My smile wrapped around my face and without even an ounce of hesitation, I said "Yes, Baby let's try this." He gave me his signature laugh but it wasn't the usual "that's my best friend laugh". It was a little more to that laugh. There was more sexiness, more sultriness in that laugh. So, I am now guessing that is the "that's my girlfriend" laugh. It was just something so different about that laugh. But I loved it. I was now talking to my boo!

Damn this had been one eventful day. It went from "I miss my friend" to "I'm talking to my man". My heart was racing and my head was spinning. This was truly the beginning of a roller coaster through a beautiful journey, but it was one that I was ready, willing, and wanting to take. I mean, here he was, an incredible surprise. I was not looking for him in that way but somehow, he found me. I didn't have to search, didn't have to look, and didn't have to wonder. I already had what was already mine, right at under my nose. I had only recently found out that he was who I was meant to be with. It just proves to me that everything happens in God's timing. Patience is a virtue and there are times when you must wait and allow things to reveal itself to you. He was my best friend. He knew my secrets, my silliness, and my craziness. He knew about my heartbreaks and heartaches, my fears and flaws, and my moods and moments. Yet, he still wanted to be in a committed relationship with me. He saw me. He didn't see an illusion or something that he thought he could change. He saw me for who I was just as I saw him. I knew that we were in for a ride but I just felt like with him, it was all worth it. I mean, how could I not?

I fell asleep so soundly and so peacefully that night. I hadn't slept that good in a long time. It was like my whole body was just so relaxed and my spirit was just full of joy and love. When I woke up, there was an email message that said "Good Morning, Baby. Hope you slept well. Have a wonderful day at work". Damn, it's official. I am "Baby" now. I walked into work skipping like I had just won the lottery. The day just seemed to go by so fast. I was ready leave work as soon as I got there. I couldn't wait until I got off work because I just had to hear his voice. Things had returned to normal and we picked up as though we never left. We had started talking all night again, writing letters all the time and just spending time building with one another. The only difference is that we were building towards something even greater than just a friendship.

That one twenty-four-hour period was just filled to capacity with so much emotion that I hardly had a chance to really sit and think. When I got a moment to just sit and absorb everything, I became so overwhelmed. After a series of failed relationships, I had decided that I was just going to stop looking and to focus more on my career, my business ventures, and my children. I had shifted my focus to looking to just letting things flow naturally. From my past experiences, I found that whenever I looked for something, I usually found it and it was always something that I did not want in the first place. The path to discovery seemed lead to a road of pain, heartache, and disappointment. So, that was definitely not a route that I was ever going to travel again.

At this point, I had just adopted a whole different motto in my life. My spirituality was intact, and I just merely said, while in meditation and in prayer, that if something is truly meant for me, then it would find me. I would no longer be in this vast quest of trying to find the "perfect" person to spend my life with. I was through investing my time and life into people who were undeserving of it. I was not going to give 100% of myself to anyone only to have it returned null and void. Those days were long gone. It was time for me to truly live my life.

Long gone were the days of merely existing, I wanted to live a life of peace, happiness, and love.

When my Zulu decided that he wanted to take our relationship further than a friendship, although I was completely elated, I was just a little nervous. It had nothing to do with him but with the fact that I had just reached a place in my life where I was completely over the nonsense of my past. I was no longer haunted by the issues of my failed relationships. I was happy and content with my emancipation from heartache. I had grown comfortable with not being in a relationship and just doing what I wanted, whenever I felt like it. I was not entrapped by the confines of relationship etiquette or having to incorporate anyone else in my life. I was free to come and go as I pleased. I was free to do what I wanted. Relationships can be so complexed, so full of challenges. I was finally free of all of that. I just wasn't sure if I was ready to jump back in and start up something new. I don't know if that was out of fear or what. I have always been the relationship type. I have always valued monogamy. But after my failed relationships, I became a little more cautious, a little more careful. I knew what I wanted. I just did not want to fail.

My sit down with myself took me through a range of emotions. The journey through my mind took me through so many incidents. No, it wasn't pleasant but it was necessary. I had to sort some things out. I was about to embark on an amazing journey with someone who I loved dearly and I owed it to him to give him my all. I wanted a healthy, happy, long-lasting relationship with Zulu and that meant ridding myself of anything that could be toxic to what we were building. He offered me everything, his love, his loyalty, and his life. Because he did and I was willing to accept it, he deserved my all as well. I was going to have to completely reciprocate that sentiment. You can only demand what you are willing to give. You can't expect someone to give you 100% if you are only going to give them 50%. We were building a foundation of equality and stability. I was not going to make him pay for the mistakes of those from my past. I was not going to bring in any emotional baggage. I was going to be free; mind, heart, and spirit. Free to love and be loved.

I went back and forth in my mind. But you know what? Life is all about choices. It is all about what you make of it. You can't walk around in hesitancy simply because of fear. There are times when you must take chances; you must take that leap of faith. You can't live in the shadows and horrors of your past and expect to have a bright future forward. How can you concentrate on moving forward if you are still looking backwards? There comes a time when you must face your fears head on, conquer old demons, and enjoy the precious gift of life. Each lesson that you learn in life is meant to prepare you for the next step in the journey. I had gotten so used to the comfort of certainty that I was complacent. My ignorance was truly my bliss. My relationship with Zulu was about to change everything that I had grown to know to be comfortable. It was about to test everything that I thought I would no longer have to worry about. I was ready and so was he. I was ready to take that chance and a leap of faith and to live, not just exist. I looked up and realized that it was almost time for me to head home. I was so at peace, so ready to begin this journey with my sweetheart.

On the ride home, I turned up my music and was just enjoying riding through my city. I felt so light, unstressed, unbothered. I was just ready to hear my honey's country voice! I had so much that I wanted to talk about, so much that I wanted to say. Not to mention, I had to plan my visit. Now I had seen my Zulu through hundreds of pictures but I had yet to see him in person. I was waiting for the day that I would be able to hug and kiss this man. I was so ready to just touch his handsome face, hold on to his big strong hands, and kiss those juicy lips. But for right now, I was just waiting for the phone to ring. I needed that fix of hearing his voice. So, I headed home to wait for that call and 15 minutes later, there was my baby!

Chapter 2

The Whirlwind Romance

My relationship with Zulu was on a swift, steady pace down lover's lane. We were talking and building with one another on a consistent basis. We were exchanging letters almost every day of the week, and he would call as often as he could. We were getting acquainted with one another and just taking the time to really get to know each other on an even more enhanced level. When you have been just friends with someone and you elevate that relationship into something more, you must learn that person on a more intimate level. The depth of your relationship changes as you are getting to learn each other in a different capacity. In turn, you now have to incorporate what you are learning and building together into a meaningful and sustainable relationship. Learning, knowing, and understanding all those things are necessary for a successful relationship.

It is important to really get to know the person that you are building a life with. So much had happened during the time that we were not in touch. There were breakups, adjustments, and just the overall hustle and bustle of everyday life. Although those things occurred within a brief period, all those attributes have come to shape the type of people that we have become now. Everything that you experience in life is lesson learned. You can choose to learn from it and grow or to just ignore it and continue in your own ignorance. Nevertheless, it was important that we found out all that we needed to know about one another, besides; we were building a relationship together. Our romance was budding into something beautiful, something incredible.

Time was flying by fast for us. We had just reconnected a few days ago and all we had been doing is talking, laughing, and laying the foundation for our relationship. Our relationship was blossoming into something beautiful and treasured. We were both attentive, understanding, and encouraging. It was everything that I could have ever imagined. The only thing that was hard to get around was location. People in ordinary relationships have the comfort of spending time together and doing things like taking walks in the park, having candlelight dinners, and long, unending conversations. We were not able to have that opportunity due to his incarceration so that meant that we had to do things a little differently. We had to get resourceful and creative.

Our relationship is what I would like to call "extraordinary". Our effort of spending time together was confined to letters and phone calls. Through those channels we did so much laughing, joking, and talking. We would spend hours just asking and answering questions, sharing stories, and reflecting on past experiences. While we had all the makings of a traditional, face-to-face relationship, the circumstances surrounding it were completely unconventional. Because of that fact, we had to make every moment that we shared with one another count. Every moment was precious and we didn't have any to waste. It was at this point in our relationship that I learned what it meant to truly cherish the small things. I took nothing for granted; I didn't have the luxury to. What would seem so *small and so insignificant to others was full of relevance to me. I cherished everything; the phone calls, the cards, the letters, the smile on his face, the smell of his cologne, and the softness of his tone. I believe that the fact that we spent so much time getting to know each other and that we were friends first is what made our relationship as strong and as meaningful as it is now.*

With November in full bloom and a romance made in heaven, Zulu decided that it was time to take our relationship to the next level, to the highest plateau. I have experienced heartache and heartbreak in my life and although I knew that he was not like anyone from my past relationships, there was a little anxiety because I knew what that plateau meant. I had to be sure that he was ready and in fact, if I was ready. Sometimes, we get wrapped up in the feeling of being ready and forgetting what being ready actually is. With everything that has happened in the past few days, we were amid a beautiful whirlwind romance. I mean, it was incredible, more beautiful than I would or could have ever dreamed. Although I had no reason to think otherwise, I just wanted us both to be sure that we were ready. Part of me wanted to just take slow steps and proceed cautiously while the other part of me just want to cast caution into the wind and just go with the flow. Besides, you only live once, right?

I am sure that he sensed some anxiety on my part. Not because he felt like I didn't love him, but because of the things that I experienced in my past. He knew my story and the hauntings from my past relationships. Trust and commitment was everything to me. Some of the heartbreak and pain that I experienced had been related to those two issues. So I wanted to be extremely careful before I jumped in all over again. I didn't want to experience anything like that again. However, I knew that I did not want to be shackled by the pain of my past. I had no reason to doubt his words and feelings. I can only go by what I saw and how I felt. I could only go on what he showed me. Now, Zulu has always been the proving type. So, I knew that he was going to prove in some way that he was ready to take this relationship further. He was going to continue to make his feelings clear to me. It is one thing to sit and tell someone something or to write those words in a letter, at this point it was about action. I wanted him to show me that he was worthy of my love and that he wouldn't abuse it.

Because Zulu is the type of man that I have always knew that he was, he was hell bent on proving to me that our relationship was strong, solid, and permanent. He wanted me to know that he was in this for the long haul. I will never forget that beautiful November day, November 13th to be exact. I had gone through my day as normal, a 12-hour work day and then home to get the kids all squared away. Homework was being done, dinner was cooking, and I was getting myself prepared for the next work day. I was in full Mommy mode. After which, I was looking forward to spending evening relaxing with my Honey. I was exhausted from the day so by the time my phone rang, I was already out of the shower and in bed looking at T.V.

My Honey's voice was just as calm and soothing as usual. After asking me about my day at work and me asking him about his day, he got quiet for a few seconds. It was a brief pause. So then he says "Hey Baby, I got a question for you?" I could sense it was something major. So, I sit up in the bed and say, "Sure Babe, what is it?". And then he says "Would you do something for me?" I am like "Yeah Hun, What's up?" That is when he said the most unforgettable words in the world. In his sexy, country voice, he said "Would you spend the rest of your life with me? Will you marry me, Shelle?" I was completely speechless for about a second, which was long enough for me to catch my breath before I started screaming "Yes, Yes, Yes!" I was so happy, completely overjoyed. Tears began to flow freely from my eyes for these were the most beautiful words that I have ever heard. Here it was, I was just minding my own business. I was focusing on my career and my kids and not even worrying about any man. I was content with just living on my own terms. I had no idea that he would be the one that I was going to spend the rest of my life with. I was not looking for anyone, not to mention him and here it is that he found me. I was elated. My Zulu was everything that I have ever wanted in a mate. I mean, he couldn't be more "perfect" for me. Like I said before, he has always been one to prove his point and he did that! He proved exactly what the highest plateau meant. He just meant I was going to be his wife. And he made it official after 1 WEEK! Just last week he was my friend and now he is about to be my husband. He went from "Buddy" to "Baby" in one damn week! Needless to say, my Honey wasn't playing any games. Time waits for no one and he proved that to damn sure be true.

I was so happy to be engaged to him. But even with the happiness, I had some things that I had to figure out for myself. I had already been married before, I was still in

*progressing and transitioning in my career, and I was
planning to start my own business. With those things and
my children, I was just bogged down. There was so much on
my plate at the time and now there was the added fact that
I was marrying a man that was in prison. Even with all of
the love and happiness that I felt at that moment, I stopped
and wondered how my life was going to change now that I
was about to be married again. I wondered how I was
going to fulfill all of the duties to the roles in my life and
still have time for myself. Regardless to everything that I
had going on, I still could not forget about me. My mind
was racing at a hundred miles a minute.*

*Here I was finally engaged to the man of my dreams
and I have so much going on with myself. I think the biggest
fear at that point was being afraid that I wouldn't have the
time to be the wife that he needed, the wife that he
deserved. I was afraid that being married was going to
postpone the plans that I had set for my own life. Although I
loved Zulu, I did not want to lose myself into just being his
wife and mother to our children. It is so much more to me
than just that. There were still desires, dreams, and goals
that I wanted to fulfill and I did not want to stop my
mission. I had plans and deadlines that I wanted to meet
and I was just a little nervous now that I am about to
become a wife. I had to figure out how I was going to
handle it all. I was beginning to stress and I decided that I
had to consult a higher power. I had to go to the one that
knew me the best and could get me through my worst. I had
to consult with God.*

*While I am not merely as religious as I should be, I
am spiritual enough to love, believe, trust, know, and*

understand God. I believe in His word and I know that He is never going to put more on me than I can bear. He will always lead me and guide me to the path in which I am to take. So, I prayed and asked God to show me the way to go, to order my steps, and to give me the wisdom and understanding that I needed. I stopped worrying and started being receptive. I knew that whatever God brought me to, that He was going to bring me through. Zulu was a gift from Him. Though Zulu, I could see God's true love for me. This man was sent to heal, restore, and protect me with his very own life. He was sent to be my peace, my strength, my comfort, someone that I could trust, someone that would love me unconditionally. Because God blessed me such a precious gift, surely, He would bless me with everything that I needed to care for and nurture it. It was then that I got the answers to everything that I needed. I knew that everything was going to be fine and that I could still do all the things that I had to do and still be the wife that he needed. I wanted to continue to be the best mom to my boys. I couldn't and wouldn't ever slight them under any circumstance. Zulu has always been encouraging and supportive with any and everything that I have ever wanted to do. And hell, I could multi-task. All of this was an epiphany of sorts. And with that, I knew that accepting his proposal was the best thing that I could have ever done.

A few days after my engagement, I finally got the call that I was waiting for. I got approved for visitation. Goodness, I was about three minutes from passing out. I was about to have the chance that I had been waiting on since I first met him. I am going to get to see him. I will be able to touch him, hug him, and kiss him. Just the thought of kissing those lips had my heart doing somersaults between my lungs. I was just a big ball of emotion. But one thing for certain is that, I was ready. Since my fiancé was in Macon, Georgia, there was a 10-hour ride ahead of me. I honestly didn't care if he was 20-hours away. There is nothing that would have stopped me from getting to my Honey. All I wanted to do was to get to my Zulu. Everything else was just a matter of minor detail. So, when the following Thursday came, I got myself ready to head to Georgia. That meant taking a nap, gassing up the car, packing clothes, getting my playlist together, saying my prayers and heading on out on my 10-hour drive. I was driving down alone but the fact that he could call made the trip even more pleasant. I love driving so this was no chore for me. Besides, I looked forward to the time alone and away from the monotony of everyday life. So much was happening so fast, I just needed a minute to take everything in. Driving would definitely give me that opportunity.

My very first visitation was probably the most life-changing experience in the world. First, there was the agony of dealing with those tedious forms. That was followed by being searched, patted down, scrutinized, and screened. The crap that you have to deal with is enough to make you feel violated and frustrated. But, I did not let that deter my mood. I was there for one purpose and one purpose only and that was to spend time with my Zulu. This was such a momentous visit. It was more than just going in and having a conversation with someone. I was about to see my future husband, the man that I was going to spend the rest of my life with. I was entering a piece of what would be my world until my husband is released. This would be the place that I would have to spend my holidays, birthdays, and anniversaries. This would be the place that I would get married. The thought of that made me sad. The same reason I love the place is the same reason that I hate it. But on the flip side, this is where the love of my life is. This is where I met my better half, where I would be building and strengthening my relationship. And although I pulled up to this place and went in with that anxiety, I knew that this was just temporary. This place was not going to define my relationship or our worth as individuals. This place did not create the love that we have for one another so I would not allow it to dictate how we chose to live our lives. This place was simply a temporary location in a permanent situation. What we have, what we have created, and what we are building is permanent. This location is only temporary.

When I walked into the visitation room, I was more nervous than a hooker in church. I was tired from the drive but I was there and it was all that mattered. The visitation room had other guys and their visitors in there. They were laughing, talking, and just enjoying the time with their loved ones. When I sat at my assigned table, I dropped my head down and said a prayer. I needed something to calm my nerves and since the vending machine does not sell vodka, I was going to have to rely on meditation and prayer. I dozed off for like one minute when I heard this extremely familiar voice says "So, are you going to get up and hug me?" I looked up and there was the love of my life standing over top of me. I fought back every urge that I had to cry. I was just too cute and you know I had to be extra. I got up and hugged my Honey and kissed those lips. Whew!

That was a moment that I have waiting and dreaming for forever! And it was worth the wait and that long ass drive. All the preparing, planning, nervousness, and anxiety had gone right out the window at the one moment.

Sitting across from my Honey, sneaking in kisses, holding hands, and looking into his eyes had to be one of the most amazing feelings in the world. And then, he does the absolute cutest thing. He reached into his pocket and gave me my first gift, a Jolly Rancher. It was the sweetest, gesture in the world. He told me that he wanted to give me something that was just as sweet as me. He loves Jolly Ranchers. So, the fact that he wanted to share his precious candy with me was just so cute. Me and my sentimental self, I never ate the Jolly Rancher, I kept it. I put it away and I have never eaten it. I guess it meant so much to me. I think it was what it symbolized. I am a symbolistic type person so just knowing that he was willing to give me something that he loved meant so much to me. Yes, call me a teddy bear but I will be that way when it comes to my love.

How did I get here? How did I get to this point in my life when everything made sense? Here it is we started out as the best of friends. That friendship has developed into a relationship and we are soon-to-be married. I knew that we were in for a ride but at that moment, I knew that there was no one in the world that I would rather take this journey with. Although I knew that my decision to marry him was going to be filled with judgement, misunderstanding, ridicule, and questions by others, none of that changed the way that I felt about him. My relationship with Zulu was between God, him, and me. Therefore, the thoughts and opinions of others were just not my concern. I just felt like if I could deal with my situation, then I would be fine. I didn't feel the need to have to justify my decision to be with him to anyone. I am sitting in front of this amazing man, filled with love, charisma, understanding, loyalty, determination, and strength who seeks only my love, loyalty, and devotion to him. This man loves me not out fear or desperation but out of a pure, sacred love that was placed upon him by God. All he wants to do is love me and to have me reciprocate that love to him. How can I lose? Now although we knew that we were going to go through some things and weather some storms, the foundation that we were building was strengthening to withstand it all.

After 6 blissful hours, it was time for me to leave. That was the hardest thing to do. So, when it was time to go, I stood up, kissed him, and hugged him tight. Tears just started to flow and there was no fighting them back. How am I supposed to do this? When will this get easier? How do I leave half of my heart? But then he looked at me, wiped my tears and said, "This will all be over sure enough, Baby". I am coming home to you very soon". He kissed me again and I walked away. I waved, blew him a kiss, and left. As I walked back through the gates alone, all I heard was the clicking, buzzing, and locking of the doors and gates. It was just so crazy that the man that I love is encased in this hell hole of wires and bars. He was so close but yet still so far. I continued my walk and when I got to my car, I started to cry. I know that this is hard on me so I can only imagine how he must feel. My heart felt like it was bleeding. I knew I had to be strong. I knew that whatever came with this, I would have to endure. Nothing in life worth having comes *easy. I looked in the mirror, dried my eyes, and called to check in on my sons. After hanging up with them, I took a deep sigh, and whispered my Honey's name. Just right before I put the phone down to begin my drive, my phone began to ring. My face lit up as soon as I heard the automated recording. After pushing the number 5 and accepting the call, I hear the words "Hey, Baby". There he was. It was like he knew I was calling out for him. I connected the phone to the car's Bluetooth, fastened my seatbelt, and began my long journey back to Virginia.*

Our First Visitation
November 2015

Chapter 3

The Two Become One

First comes love, then comes marriage......Now that we were engaged, it was time to start planning for our big day. Contrary to what some people may believe, preparing for a marriage at a prison is not a simple task. It's not just a walk-in, sign your name on a piece of paper in front of the prison chaplain and then you are married. There is so much that you have to do to prepare for that special day. Just because the confines of the prison wall exist, there were still things that we could do to make the wedding day special. Yet, everything had to be planned and completed in steps. The first step was to apply for marriage. Because inmates are considered to be in custody of the state, they have to apply with the prison to be married. After the approval process, you are given a selection of dates to be married. Zulu and I couldn't wait to be married so we were going to take the first date that they had available. I had to find a pastor, get the marriage license, speak to his counselor and the prison chaplain, and have paperwork sent into the prison by the clerk to be signed and notarized. That is in addition to finding something to wear, get rings, write vows, and make an appointment to get my hair and nails done. It was really time to get busy. There was no time to waste.

As with any wedding day, you want your day to be special. Your wedding day is a memorable showcase of the love, devotion, and commitment of two people. Just because a marriage takes place is a prison does not mean that it is less meaningful or less stressful. I wanted everything to be so beautiful and so intimate. There is only so much allowed so we had to make the best of the situation. The weeks leading up to the wedding were one adventure after another.

There were so many delays and mishaps that I just broke down and cried. I even questioned if it was even meant for us to be married. It seemed like everything was just standing in the way of me getting our marriage license. I remember the first time I went to DeKalb County to get the marriage license. When I got there, the clerk told me that the signature from the prison's notary was in the wrong place. That meant that the form was null and void. It also meant that I was going to have to mail everything back in, wait for him to be called out to see the notary, and have the form sent back. We were getting married in a week and time wasn't on our side. I live in Virginia and he is in Georgia so the average mail time was about 3 to 4 days. I had begun to freak out. As soon as I got in the car, I just sat there in complete disbelief. It seemed as if he could feel that something was wrong with me. Moments later, Zulu called me as I was sitting in front of the courthouse and I just broke down in tears. He sat there just listening to me cry and he said to me "Baby, God is going to work all of it out".

I called up to the counselor and told her the situation. She told me to just come on up and she would do the paperwork over for me. I was just elated. It was a two-hour drive but I was not willing to leave Georgia without it. The weather had gotten bad; it was raining, windy, thundering, and lightning. It was now dark and I was starting to lose signal on my GPS. All I could do was pray. I *guess God heard my prayers because I made it all the way to the prison without incident. As soon as I pulled up at the prison, Zulu called. I really needed to talk to him. I needed his reassurance and his gentleness. I was a complete bucket of tears earlier. But as always, he knew exactly what to say to ease my anxieties and discomfort. Just as I had finally calmed down, the counselor showed up and told him to get dressed and come with her so she could re-sign the paperwork. I was so grateful. So, by 10 p.m., my papers had been re-signed. Now I would have a long trip back to Virginia because I had to work the next morning, but just knowing that I was going to be able to get my marriage license was worth it all. Just as promised, God worked it out. I headed back to the highway on my journey to Virginia with a calm spirit. I was a tired spirit, but definitely a calm one.*

Zulu was excited and nervous at the same time. However, he would never admit to being nervous. With each step of the wedding process, I would ask him "Are you nervous, Baby?" He would answer each and every time with a smile and then say "No". I know he was lying but I guess he just didn't want me to know. I guess his cool ass was just too smooth for that. He was not about to admit that the idea of spending the rest of his life with this 5 foot 6 inches of pure caramel colored awesomeness was making his tall, strong ass a little nervous. For as long as I have known him, he has always been so strong, so rooted, and so focused but deep inside; I knew he was shaking like a leaf. His lil' stomach was full of butterflies. I mean, he was about to take a major step in his life and I can understand how that could make anyone anxious. Hell, even I was edgy. But, his cool ass refused to show any signs of nervousness. Well, at least not to me, anyways.

So, when one of his brothers called me and told me that he had been out running the track for half the day, couldn't help to laugh. First of all, who the hell runs the track almost all day? Not even the world's famous sprinters and track stars run all damn day. Now, my Zulu has always been the athletic type but we all knew that he was running those nerves down. He wasn't fooling anybody. My baby was out there with sparks coming from them Nikes. I mean, at this point, we were down to the last few days before our wedding. So having those pre-wedding jitters was normal. I was only holding on to an ounce of sanity myself. With everything that had happened and the whole debacle in DeKalb, I had been a complete emotional wreck. I was waiting for the day that we finally got married so that all of this would be over with and we could move on with our "Happily Ever After".

I had finally arrived back to Virginia, but I would only be home for about one day before I started out for my wedding weekend. It was the Wednesday night before our wedding on Friday and I needed to rest. I had a long drive the next night. I had to work on Thursday morning so sleep was a must. But you know, sometimes your mind and your body do not always agree. My body was telling me that I needed to rest but my mind was going a million miles a minute. All I could think about was making sure that I had everything that I needed and getting to the prison on time. I had a 10-hour drive and had to be at the prison by 11 a.m. so I did not have the luxury to forget anything or to be late. With everything that I had to do, you would think that I

43

would just fall right to sleep. That was so not the case. My mind just wouldn't let me rest and my anxiety level was higher than the clouds.

I looked at my dress and wedding bands for the umpteenth time. It was just something about my dress that just made everything so real. For the past few months, I had been just floating on this cloud, just soaring through my day-to-day. There was so much preparation and processing to prepare for this day that I honestly just felt like I was floating in the wind. Even with the debacles and mishaps, I still felt like it was all a dream, like I was having some major out of body experience. For some reason, looking at my dress and the wedding bands just made it all real. In a matter of hours, my life was about to change, I would be standing there in front of God, Zulu, and our judge, pledging to spend the rest of my life with him. I would become his wife, his better half and he would become mine. I would bear the beautiful responsibility of honoring my vows to the man that God himself took the time and created just for me. I would become personally responsible and accountable for the care and concern of his heart and spirit. And knowing that, truly taking the time to understand this path that God has placed before me, all of my nervousness began to subside. It was like this overwhelming warm peace brushed upon me and I was now able to relax. So, I packed all the accessories, went over my vows, counted the fee for the judge, and made sure that I was sure to stash my marriage license in my Bible. I rechecked my bags, made sure that I had everything in the truck, and went back in the house.

My phone began to ring and it was my Zulu. I was checking for all signs of nervousness and although I listened hard, there was still no sign of the butterflies. He hid those things very well. We talked and laughed and just enjoyed each other. Before we ended our phone call, he said to me, "All I ever wanted is for someone to love me the way that I love them and Baby, you have done just that and that's why I am marrying you." I didn't say anything but tears began to flow from my eyes. Damn, I am such a marshmallow for this man. I can honestly say that I have never been this happy in my life before. I have so much peace, so much joy, and more love than I have ever known. So, after the phone hung up, I went to the shelf and pulled out my basket of letters from him. I have kept ever single letter, card, picture, and envelope that he has ever sent me. I looked over at his picture, started reading his letters and finally I drifted off to sleep. His words have always had that soothing effect on me. He has always written just as if he was talking to me so having those letters was exactly what I needed since I was unable to verbally speak to him. And it was exactly what I needed to fall asleep. Besides, I was marrying the love of my life the next day and I wanted to be well-rested, bright eyed, and beautiful for my big day.

Thursday night was gone and the sun had come up on my big day. I had been on the highway the entire night. As I drove, I could see the beautiful sunrise before me on this incredible day. I was due to reach my hotel by 7:30 a.m. and I had time to take me a nap before I began getting dressed for my wedding. I was required to be at the prison by 11 a.m. and not a minute later. There was only a 20-minute drive from the hotel to the prison so I had plenty of time to catch me a nap. So, after checking into the hotel and getting to my room, I set my alarm and drifted off to sleep. Right before the alarm went off, my phone began to ring. And guess who that was? Yup, my husband-to-be had awakened me from my sweet slumber.

I laid there for those 15 minutes talking to him and mentally preparing myself for what was about to happen. I just had to know so I asked him for the final time, "Baby, are you nervous yet?" When he said "Yeah, a little bit but you know it ain't no pressure though, boo". His Georgia slang is just plain funny to me. But he was nervous. Here it is "Mr.-I–don't-get-nervous", nerves was all tore up. I have no idea why that made me smile. I guess it was the fact of what it symbolized to me. He is always so strong, so collected, and so calm about everything. But for that moment, he showed me that although he is all those things, he is still human and comfortable with expressing and exposing his vulnerabilities and anxieties to me without fear of judgement. Hell, I am sure that even Superman has gotten nervous before. I mean, I would be scared to damn death if I had to run into a burning building. Honestly, I was also secretly glad that it wasn't just me who was the nervous wreck. I had been through a roller coaster of emotions getting ready for this day.

During our conversation, I looked over at the clock and went into complete panic mode. I was worried about everything. My pre-wedding jitters were in overdrive. I was a half of second from losing my damn mind. I was just extra. I was worried about my dress, my hair, and everything in between. Just when I was about to pass out from a manic overload, he said to me, in the calmest,

sweetest voice ever "Just get up here and marry me, Lady".
There it was again, that calm that he just breathed right
into me. With those words, my phone call ended and I
began to get dressed to go and marry the love of my life.

I jumped into the shower, and called to check on the
kids to make sure that they were getting ready for school.
They were supposed to be leaving out of the door before
8am. After I hung up with them, suddenly time had begun
to fly. I had to do my make-up, get dressed, and prepare
myself to be sane for the 20-minute drive to the prison.
After getting completely dressed and looking in the mirror,
my nerves kicked into high gear again. I was standing there
in the mirror, making sure that I looked completely
flawless. I wanted to look perfect for my husband-to-be. Just
as I was getting into the car, I started getting bombarded
with so many calls. My Facebook notifications were going
haywire. Our friends and family members were calling to
wish us well and to see if we had already gotten married. It
was a much needed distraction for a little while but as I got
closer to the prison, I turned off my phone and began to
pray. I needed God to speak to me; I needed to hear a word
from Him to know that I was doing something that was
going to be both pleasing and a blessing.

My prayer was simple. I asked God to bless us on our
marriage and to guide our lives in the direction that leads
us closer to Him and each other. Having God at the head of
our marriage was and is important to both Zulu and I, for
we knew that it was absolutely necessary for our marriage
to be blessed and for its survival. We were entering into a
marriage that is statistically doomed to fail. If we were
going to beat those odds, we were going to have to trust,

believe, and depend on God and one another. He was going to have to be at the head of our marriage if we were going to succeed. We had to hold tight to one another, to be able to weather the storms of life, to celebrate in our successes, and learn from our failures together. Marriage is about accepting the perfect imperfections of our life's mate and building a foundation on which we will grow and develop together. We decided a long time ago that failure and divorce was not an option for us. We were completely devoted to each other and to making this marriage work. And, we were committed to doing whatever it took to make our marriage a healthy, happy, and lasting one.

I finally pulled into the parking lot of the prison at 10:35 a.m. I was nervous and excited at the same time. I asked God one more time to please give me a sign if I was making a mistake. I mean, I wanted something drastic to happen just so I would know that it was a sign from him, like my heel on my shoe breaking or all the alarms ringing and doors of the prison opening up. I wanted a big sign. To my delight, there were no flukes or mishaps. Everything was as smooth as silk. On the walk to the Administration Building, I felt like the wind was pushing me closer with each step. It almost felt as if I was floating on air. I knew at that moment, that marrying Zulu was my destiny. Walking up and through the parking lot seemed like it took seconds instead of minutes. Never in my life had I been so nervous before. I had taken that walk and entered that visitation room so many times before now. But this walk seemed more meaningful and more purposeful. I was about to embark on another chapter in my life. Today I walked in a *single lady but I was going to be leaving as a married woman. I am a Queen, about to marry my King.*

My life was about to change and I was about to begin a journey that would guide me to be the woman that I knew that I could be. Everything that I had wanted was about to happen. After years of failed relationships and past hurts, I had finally had the love, peace, and happiness that I had be craving all those years ago. I finally had what I knew I deserved. It was just a matter of standing and waiting on God. Sometimes we sabotage things by jumping the gun and acting in our own timing. We have to be in such a rush to get what we want and end up getting worse than what we expected. But, we must wait on God. We must rely on Him and understand that when He wants it to happen, it will. We cannot rush a blessing. We cannot do His work. Our job is to stand in patience, step out on faith, and trust that His will is done. And just as always, God was right on time. No longer was I going to be victim to hurt, pain, and disappointment. I was no longer bounded and shackled by my painful past. I was finally free to love and to be loved. This beautiful day had finally come. I was going to marry the man that I was destined to be with, the man that taught me the true meaning of love. This man has shown and proved that love is indeed patient and kind. On that beautiful day in May at 12:12p.m., I kissed my husband and began that journey.

Our Wedding Day
Introducing Mrs. Hooper

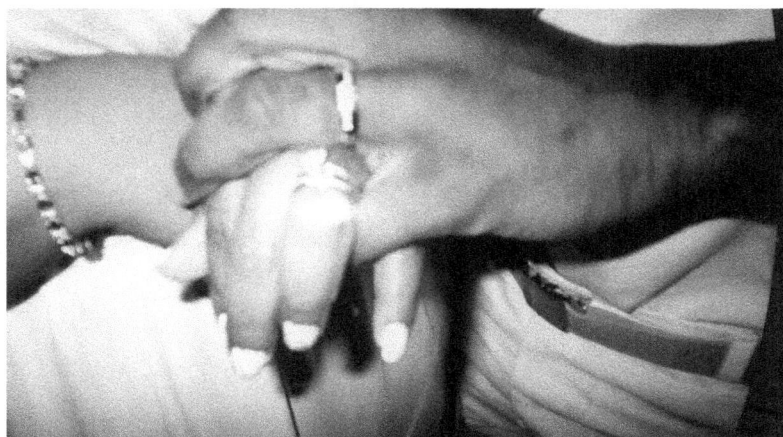

Chapter 4

Our First Year of Togetherness

After the wedding, there is the honeymoon period. All of the stress of the wedding was over and it was time to get on with the business of living as husband and wife. I was moving up steadily in my career, the kids were doing great, and Zulu was in school and working. Visitations, letters, and phone calls were rolling and on schedule. Everything was going great. My husband and I were making wonderful strides in our relationship. We were closer than ever and loving each other more and more with each passing day. I didn't think that things could get any better, other than his release from prison. The calendar was flipping constantly and time was flying by. It just seemed that we couldn't get enough of one another. We were experiencing all of the attributes of honeymoon bliss. We were still building, growing, and developing. We were both working on various projects and exploring different business avenues. To some, the fact that we were preparing for our future seemed strange because of his incarceration but we know that planning is essential. Like my husband says "Proper preparation prevents poor performance." We lived by that quote. All in all, married life was just wonderful.

The first year brings about so many changes. All of the hype and hoopla of the big day is over with and now you are married. You are now joined together as husband and wife for what is supposed to be forever. You are learning even more about the other person. You are learning how to connect your lives together and incorporate each other completely into the other person's world. The transition was a relatively smooth one but just as with life in general, there are sometimes a few bumps in the road. But the bottom line is that you are married now and the rules change a whole lot when you get married. There are a lot of people who don't get that. They still want to conduct themselves as though they were just dating, not understanding that you must put in even more work to sustain a marriage. The same things that you did in the beginning of the relationship are not going to be enough to sustain it. To grow, you must change. Things are not just going to stay the same. Marriage is work. It takes time and patience, compromise and understanding, forgiving and loving, and kindness and gentleness. Marriage is about understanding that the person that you married is the person that you pledged to spend the rest of your life with; good, bad, or indifferent. The fact that the other half is in prison does not make you immune from the worries, issues, cares, and concerns of life. In fact, you have to work even harder because you don't have the luxuries of the both of you being physically in each other's presence.

No marriage or relationship comes without bumps and bruises. Marriage is not all about sunny skies and beautiful rainbows, each and every day. My husband and I have experienced our fair share of trials and tribulations, but we have gotten through those things by communicating, praying, and gravitating towards one another even more. We decided a long time ago that "divorce" was never ever going to be an option. We took that off the table. When we decided that we wanted to get married, stand before God, and pledged ourselves to one another until "death do us part", we meant it. So everything that happened in between the journey of life and death was going to be something that we were going to have to deal with together. We were going to hold on to that three stranded cord and keep it pushing. By the grace of God, we have succeeded so far. But you know what? This is just a little bit of the test, kind of like the pre-test. The real test is going to begin when he comes home. That is when it is really going to get real. No longer will we be guarded and confined by the walls of the prison. We will be free to do things our own way, in our own time, with different challenges, temptations, and influences consistently around us. Now coupled with the fact that you are dealing with a person who has just been sitting in a place where they are told what to do, when to do it, how to do it, and confined to one space, there are going to be some hurdles. I am not saying that there is going to be infidelities and the other major issues like that but it is important that a marriage is built and nurtured on a strong, solid foundation. That is absolutely a must to withstand the test that will come.

As I said before, there are no marriages that are immune from the difficulties of life. Even in my marriage, I have experienced difficulties, from Facebook stalkers and haters to ex-girlfriends still trying to hang on. Yes, there were times that my patience and my religion was tested. I know that I have thought about slapping me a few people because of their need to insert their opinions about me and my marriage or to hold on to memories with my husband. My desire to not want to go to prison myself may have been the only thing that saved some people from feeling my raft.

There were plenty of times that I would have to stop and check myself and ask myself questions like "If I slap this hoe and she call the police on me, who is gonna pick up my kids from football practice?" Or, "Will they sell my favorite cereal on commissary?" And even more importantly, "Will me running over this bitch with my car keep me from seeing my husband and kids?" I thank God every day for giving me a soothing spirit because if it wasn't for Him, I am sure that a couple of people would have come up short. I am so glad that I digressed though. Nevertheless, all marriages experience issues. It is not about pointing fingers and assigning blame. It is about communication, forgiveness, and getting through each ordeal. It is about keeping your marriage between the two of you and working on getting back on the same accord.

Zulu and I happen to be both thinkers and strategists. Our systematic approach to marriage is what has allowed us to build and sustain our marriage. Now although we do not claim to know the answer to marriage building, we know what has worked for us. People are different and every marriage is different so what may work for some may not necessarily work for others. Everything that we do is to build up and continue to grow individually as well as with one another. Here are just a few of the principles that we follow.

1. *Never go to bed angry at one another. Any issues or disputes that we have, we try to resolve before the day is over. When you are up and constantly thinking about the mishap, it takes away from your ability to function and be productive in both your everyday routines and in*

your marriage. It also leaves that proverbial bruise on your mind and spirit, which can lead to even more of a breakdown, or an even greater disconnect in your marriage. So, our goal has always been to resolve our issue or at least discuss it to the point that we are no longer mad or grossly upset.

2. *Talk to one another; not at one another. Engage in a real conversation. A marriage is not about whose right or wrong. It is not about screaming, shouting, or trying to drive your point-of-view into someone or persuading them to do what you want. A real conversation involves taking the time to stop and listen to what the other is saying. We listen to understand, don't just listen to respond.*

3. *We are both equal. Treat each other the way that you want to be treated. Neither one of us will consider ourselves to be more significant or greater than the other. Although the natural order is that the man is the head of the family, it still is essential that we treat each other's as equals in our ways and actions. Love one another with patience and equality.*

4. *Communication is the key. Zulu and I make it a point to always communicate. It is our time to exchange our thoughts, ideas, visions, and feelings. It is our way to express ourselves to one another. We talk about any and everything. There is nothing that is off limits with us. Our conversations are our way to connect to one*

another. We are not mind readers and we don't possess any kind of psychic capability. If you don't talk about it, then how the other supposed to know what is going on? The ability to communicate alleviates misunderstandings and just serves as an overall way to strengthen and enhance our marriage.

5. *Always be respectful in your ways and actions. Respect goes a long way. Talk to your spouse with respect and kindness. Even when there is tension, remember to always be respectful and mindful of the other's thoughts, feelings, and opinions. Your job is to be the other's peace, to cherish, honor, and respect another. Avoid yelling, cursing, swearing, threatening, and intimidating your spouse. Respect goes such a long way and it is earned and not given. There are honestly times when my husband irks my nerves, and I know I can do the same with him but we are always sure to treat each other with respect and kindness.*

6. *Compromising is not the enemy. Compromising does not mean accepting defeat, giving in, or bowing down. Compromise simply means coming to a mutual understanding and working on a way to incorporate the wishes of the both of you into one common goal. There will be times when you have to agree to disagree. You may not always agree on the same things but there must be some healthy medium. Understand that this is not always easy, but it is possible. Zulu*

and I have been great with that and because we have, things have been smooth. We both get what we want without alienating the other. Be selfless.

7. *Trust is everything. Just because a spouse is incarcerated does not mean that there cannot be trust issues. Our spouses are in some way connected to the outside world. We live in a society that has advanced technologically and because of that, our loved ones have more access to the outside world. Those interactions with those on the outside can create a source of tension when the other party attempts to or steps within the confines of your marriage. It is at that point when you must trust that your spouse will be respectful and honor you and your marriage. That faith and belief in your spouse is essential to a long-lasting relationship. Trust that your partner will create a boundary with others and not allow anyone to cross it and if that person does, they will be immediately cut off. Always hold marriage at the highest regard. Preserve and protect it from anyone or anything that threatens or seeks to destroy it.*

8. *Romance and Intimacy. Although my husband is incarcerated, we have ways to be intimate and connect with one another in amazing ways. We are limited to what we can do physically, but something as simple as a hug and an endearing kiss can connect you in ways that you could never even imagine. My week could be total hell*

but once I am in my husband's arms, I totally forget it all. I just lose myself in his strong embrace and energize my soul with his lips. Continually date your spouse, send letters, cards, emails, and pictures that just ooze with spice and romance. Get creative and always make the other feel needed, wanted, and desired. Shower them with love, and when you can, get in plenty of hugs and kisses. Just know that as soon as I see my husband, he is going to feel my love. And maybe a little more if I can sneak it in.

9. *Always be willing to forgive. Marriage is not always sunshine and rainbows. We are not perfect and we make mistakes. When your spouse does something to hurt, or offend you, be willing to forgive them. Accept their apology and forgive them. Truly forgive them and move on. Don't hold onto the past hurt or create a grudge. Don't bring the incident back up later or make rude innuendos or insinuations. Forgive them wholeheartedly and let it go. Understand the fact that they are not perfect and that neither are you. Oftentimes, we are offended unintentionally or due to some small misunderstanding. So be willing and quick to forgive. Now I am not saying to be so forgiving that you allow yourself to be used or be a doormat. You will know the difference. However, if your spouse does offer a sincere apology, accept it and forgive them. Forgiveness is not always easy but it is definitely necessary.*

10. *Practice the four L's: Live, Learn, Laugh, and Love. Life is already hectic enough and brings forth so many challenges. Coupled with the fact that your better half is incarcerated, it so easy to get down and depressed. Make it a point to live, not just exist but to truly live. Make every moment count. Learning is a part of growing. The two of you have incorporated your lives into one. With each of us comes a wealth of knowledge, experience, and wisdom. Embrace those things and learn from one another. Laugh all the time. Zulu and I are best friends. We laugh, joke, and play all the time. We can be as goofy and as silly as we want and have so much fun together. Our ability to laugh and enjoy each other is what makes it easier to endure the rough days that come with us being physically apart. Laughter truly is good for the soul. Love hard and unconditionally. It is always so easy to love someone when things are going good but what matters is when you love someone even when things are not so good. Be open to loving your spouse even more and then allowing them to love you as well. The fact that my husband is in prison means that I have chosen to love him despite all the reasons that society says that I shouldn't. It's about loving someone completely for who they are and not for whom you want them to be. Of course as we grow more in love, we change to the betterment of the relationship but the key is to love the person just as they are.*

Yes, we have issues but none of those issues have or will ever deter me from loving him with the very beat of my heart and what is even more beautiful is that he loves me just the same way.

11. *Pray with and for your spouse. Pray over your marriage. There is nothing more powerful than prayer and there is nothing like a praying wife. The best thing that a couple can do is pray together. Speak life, blessings, love, happiness, and peace over each other and your marriage. We had just taken those vows before God. We created that three-stranded cord and therefore every step on our path of righteousness and prosperity was going to be rooted in God and in our love and covenant to one another. I pray with and for my husband every day. I ask God to cover and protect my husband and to guide his ways, thoughts, and actions. He is in prison and although he has grown into a man of integrity and intelligence, the ills and issues of prison are around him all the time. I ask God to protect him against any and everything mentally, physically, and spiritually that could harm him. I also pray for myself. I pray that God continues to keep me covered against all negativity and to continue to allow me to be the woman that I am destined to be, and the wife that my husband needs me to be.*

12. *Keep the issues of your marriage between the two of you. Marriage is filled with joy, love, peace, and happiness. But there are also times of*

trials and turbulence. During those rough times, retreat to God and one another. Resolve your issues together, privately, and out of the way of unbiased friends and family members, and definitely away from social media. I learned a long time ago that not everyone is going to give you an unbiased opinion or are truly looking to be that shoulder to lean on. There are people and some are around you, that are hoping and praying for your demise and destruction as a couple. There are people that are sitting and waiting to say "I told you so" or "I would leave him/her" or to just gossip and blurt your business to others. Not everyone wants to see you win. Some people are just standing by to see if you have failed. Understand that family and friends are not always forgiving. You could be having a spat with your spouse, confide in someone, and all the person will ever see is that moment that you came to them in pain. You and your spouse could have had a minor disagreement and are now over it and moving on yet all the person will remember is that one time that you came to them upset. So, their view of your spouse could change and that can begin just a downward spiral of relationship breakdown as you struggle to defend your spouse. Family and friends are just not as forgiving. I have experienced this first hand in a previous relationship and nothing good came out of it. Do not go to social media to air out dirty laundry. The internet is not the place to expose your spouse or your marriage. Protect your spouse, protect your marriage, and keep others out of it.

13. *Value the opinion of your better half. Now I understand that there are times when our insecurities and feelings may overshadow things. But if your spouse comes to you and says that something that you are doing is making them unhappy, then stop and talk about it. Don't diminish their concerns. Stop and talk about it. Respect their opinions and the right to feel the way that they do. Come to some kind of mutual understanding and be willing to compromise. In some cases, that may even mean cutting and stopping some things and people off. Be willing to adjust and do what's best to keep your relationship growing and thriving. Remember, it is your responsibility to protect your spouse's heart and happiness.*

14. *This one ties into number 13 perfectly. Cut off anything and anyone that threatens the harmony, sanctity, joy, peace, and growth of your relationship. That is just as simple as it comes. Never allow anyone to disrespect or be unkind to your spouse, directly or indirectly. This includes family members and friends. Leave those exes, old trouble makers, and old party partners where they are. They have no place in your relationship. Make sure that everyone knows their place and how to stay there. Never*

invite anyone into your relationship or allow anyone to think that they are invited. If you don't feed it then it won't grow. Uninvited guest are unwanted ones. So therefore, leave their asses where they are.

15. *Provide and maintain balance. It is so easy to get tied into the everyday issues that occur in life. Because of the routines, it is so easy to start to forget to look after one another and to continue to work at your marriage. So create balance. Set time away to just focus on the two of you. Whether it's a phone call, visit, or video chat, take that time and just enjoy one another. Block out the rest of the world for a while and just give one another their time. Make each other feel needed, wanted, and appreciated. Show that love and continue to build on that foundation that you have set.*

Now understand that there is more to marriage than the 15 principles that I have mentioned above. There is so much more that goes into building and sustaining a marriage. And there are some of these points that I will elaborate on later but for the most part, these principles are what have proven themselves to be useful in our marriage. I can't speak for others and their relationships, I can only attest to mine. And so far, things have been working well in our favor.

Everything that I said has been tried and tested. Understand this, not every day is sunshine and rainbows. There are going to be days when you just love each other more than life and then there are days when you just want to ring his damn neck. There have been some days when I can't wait to hear his voice and then there are days when I answer the phone like "Oh Lord". I can't tell you how many times I have pictured lying blissfully in his arms watching TV. But I can also tell you about the times when I would have his ass sleeping on the couch. Does that mean I don't love him? Absolutely not. I love him completely. Does that mean that I am always pleasant and happy-go-lucky? Hell No. Sometimes I get on my own damn nerves. Just ask him and I am sure that he will say the same thing about me. But that is marriage. There are highs and lows, ups and downs. However, it is the most exciting, most incredible roller coaster that you will ever ride.

Marriage is a beautiful thing. You get the chance to fall in-love over and over again with the person that you know was created just for you. You get the chance to spend life with a person that knows you completely, accepts your flaws, and still loves you just as intensely and you love them. This is just our first year together and I am sure that things will happen and there will be changes and adjustment that we are going to have to make but I can honestly say that I am looking forward to the next 60 years with him. Marriage is a lifelong commitment. It is not something that should be entered into lightly or doubtfully. It is not something that you take for granted and hold with disregard. Marriage is sacred and special. As with anything that you cherish, marriage takes love, time, and patience. It takes growing, nurturing, and developing. With growth comes change. Although, we can't predict the future, we are willing to work our way towards it in the imperfect perfection of marriage. Our marriage is what we make of it. We are only going to get what we put into it. As long as we stay loyal, faithful, devoted, and committed to one another, this beautiful journey that we have chosen to take will be an everlasting one.

Chapter 5

The Blending and the Visiting

Family is very important to both Zulu and I. Now that we were married, our families were going to be blending and bonding. Our family was expanding and it was not only Zulu and I. Because I already had children from previous relationships, it was so important to me that we blended beautifully into a strong family unit. We will soon be all living in the same home and I just wanted the transition to be as smooth as possible. I had been a single parent for so long that my kids did not have to "share" me with anyone else. For so long, it was just them and I. I wondered how they were going to react now that there was going to be someone else who would share in our lives. I had plenty of conversations with my children and all of them were pleasant. I gave them the opportunity to openly and honestly voice themselves. I wanted them to their concerns, reservations, and opinions without fear of being chastised or ridiculed. I wanted them to feel completely included in our lives. Not only would my life be changing but theirs as well.

Some children have a different approach to things. The idea of having a step-parent can be too much for them to handle. They had spoken to my husband plenty of times before but they had yet to visit him. I was just amazed at the incredible bond that they had and how open and receptive they were to him. I did not have to force their relationship and he did not want to either. They just meshed together so wonderfully. Zulu made it a point to have conversations with them, encouraged them to get to know him, and to form a bond with them. He knew that he would have to gain their trust and their understanding for this to work. But he also realized how fragile that this process could be and how his current residential location would influence them and even their willingness to accept and embrace him. I felt like when we finally all got together, they would have the chance to see him and the floor would be open for them to get anything off their chest that they needed to. It would also give me the chance to be with all my guys, gauge the blending process, and to just really get a feel for the overall family dynamic. You can only imagine how happy I was when they asked to go to visitation. I mean they wanted to go. They worried me silly about going. So, I knew that this was all going to flow together harmoniously. Our family visitations were going to be wonderful.

Many people take for granted something as simple as sitting next to their spouses or having them at the dinner table or playing with the kids. The idea of calling out his or her name and having them answer is not even an afterthought. But as the wife of an incarcerated man, I am not afforded that luxury. I cannot just call out my husband's name and have him answer. There is no looking over my shoulder and seeing him standing there. There is no one to wake up in the arms of. You are essentially all alone. Visitation is a way to ease that solitude. It is the opportunity to spend some quality time your spouse, to have some sense of normalcy. Although you are under careful watch from the guards, it is time that you are otherwise not afforded. So you take nothing for granted and make the best of it.

In my opinion, prison and correctional officers along with certain rules and regulations are created to make the visitation experience as difficult as possible. While I understand that the job of the correctional officers is to provide a safe and secure environment and to maintain control of the inmates, I believe that some officers take their positions as an abuse of power. This can make the visitation experience terrible. It can also be a deterrent to keep the families from coming up to visit. Some feel like the more difficult they make the process, the more reluctant the families will be to return. Now, I am in no way a conspiracy theorist, but just my experiences during visitation causes me to think that way. There was once a time when some officers from the CERT (Correctional Emergency Response Team) stood within earshot of us throughout the entire visit. They had no reason at all to. I just felt like they were standing there to completely be irritating. But I refuse to let that undermine my purpose of being there, and that was to see my husband.

The best way that I handle it all is to just follow the rules and regulations and keep a level head. That will help you to get back to your loved ones. Any arguing or swearing can easily be grounds for you to have your visit terminated or to have your visits suspended totally. Besides, seeing my husband is the main goal and I refuse for anyone or anything to interrupt that. The time that we have is both precious and limited. So I am never going to let anyone or anything interfere with that. But believe me, I am no push over or passive and I will not tolerate any mistreatment by staff or otherwise. There is a chain of command and the Ombudsman's office where I can openly voice my concerns without interfering with my visitation. I just handle it in a way that will let them know of my disgust and displeasure while still achieving my main goal which is to spend time with my husband.

Getting prepared for visitation is not an easy task. The ride to Georgia is a 9-hour trip and that is factoring in stops for breaks to eat, use the restroom, and to get gas. There is so much preparation involved with getting there on time. Preparation starts the three days before. That includes everything from going to get quarters and making sure that they are in a clear plastic bag to making sure that there is nothing that is too tight or too revealing. I'd have to double check the boys' choices of clothes to make sure that they did not have any metal buttons or buckles or anything that would set the metal detectors off. If you are not able to clear the metal detector, then there is no entry and that would be absolutely devastating. Visitation starts 9am and ends at 3pm every weekend day and on holidays. I usually try to arrive at least by 8:30 am. That gives me enough time to get there, get processed, searched, and walked to the visitation area.

After arriving at the prison for our first official family visit, I look over and make sure that the kids are still looking their best. I sign us in and await the processing and searching. I understand that prison is not a place to take children. It is not a situation that you would voluntarily want your children to experience. The whole searching, processing, and restrictions can be overwhelming and maybe even traumatizing to children. Our children range from ages 13 to 17 years old. Although they are still young, we understand that this is not easy for them as well. It is important that we are sensitive to their feelings. We understand that it is not easy for them to have to experience the issues that go with having a parent that is in prison.

While we try to instill the family and togetherness despite our situation, we do understand that all of this can be taxing on our children. So we talk about it. We ask them what they think and how they feel. We allow them to ask questions and to speak freely about their thoughts and feelings. Having to see their father in a prison uniform, the slamming of heavy doors, buzzing in and out, the barbed wired fences, metal gates, and being sniffed by a K-9 drug detecting dog is not normal. Not being able to do all the things that normal children do with their father is hard on them. Prison not only effects the incarcerated one but it also affects their families as well.

We try our best to make visitation as less traumatic as possible. And we have been blessed to succeed at that. The children get the chance to spend quality time talking with their dad and for at least a little while, we are just like any other family. The laughs and smiles on their faces after visitation are priceless. Although we have great family visits, we do use their dad's incarceration to teach our children about the consequences of not making good choices in life. Music, videos, and social media has desensitized the views of prison. There is the unrealistic depiction that jail is a rite of passage or some sort of "hood credit". The realization of prison is not fully understood until it is something that becomes no longer a choice but a *place that you are put into by force and by the result of a choice that you made.*

We let them know that prison is a real possibility if you refuse to obey laws, rules, and regulations or conduct yourself in a way that is dangerous and detrimental to others. Prison is real. We live in a society where they are building more prisons than schools. We must teach them the realities of life. The fact that they can be incarcerated for making bad choices is real. No one is immune to the law and if you do something that is not in line with that then there are consequences, some which may include time in prison. Prison is not the glorious place that people rap about. It is not the place that you want to be. Even though we are there to enjoy our time as a family, prison is truly a place of despair and desolation and we never want them to end up there. All in all, we have great times during family visits. Talking, laughing, eating, joking, and playing games as a family gives us that time to just connect and for those few hours, there is that sense of normalcy. We make it of the utmost importance to keep the lines of communication open, laugh, love, and focus on strengthening our family bond. And that is what our family visits are all about.

During family visits, my husband and I are sure to keep our conversations limited to child-friendly topic such as school, cars, hobbies, and music but there are times when I crave that alone time with my husband. Although we are still in a visitation room, surrounded by other visitors, inmates, and correctional officers, our conversations were still just between us and they could be as intimate and as personal as we wanted them to be. We could talk about all kinds of things from sex and intimacy to planning for his release, to our visions and goals, to faith and marriage. Hand holding, touching, and kissing was not allowed, except for at the start and end of the visit. Because he is in a state that does not allow conjugal visits, which sucks tremendously, conversations were all that we have. I am just glad that they couldn't hear all our conversations because they would damn sure get an earful!

Visitation with my husband was a way for me to connect with him. We had the chance to actually see one another and to really get to know and understand one another. When you are talking over the phone, you can't see facial expressions and body language. You can only hear the change in tone. But visitation allows the opportunity to see all those things and to get the chance to learn and grow with one another. "I love you" sounds so much sweeter when you can see it coming from his lips and feels so good in the warmth of his strong but gentle embrace. I know that this in no way replaces the actual dating, courtship, and romantic evenings alone but because of our situation, we are forced to roll with the punches and make the best out of an extraordinary situation. We make the best of it. Besides, what does not kill us will only make us stronger.

I will be the first to admit that visitations are not always an uneventful time for us. We have had our arguments and disagreements quietly in the visitation room. Sometimes, they are new spats and at other times, they are a spill-over from the hours or day before. I can recall one argument we had; it was a real spill-over. We were fussing about something; I don't even remember what it was about now when I think about it. That is how silly it was. But once I got to visitation, I sat out to make sure that he understood my displeasure with whatever we were arguing about. We fussed for about an hour, well I fussed and he listened, rather. He fussed and I would listen. Although it was only an hour, it was just entirely too much time to be fussing over something that I can't even remember now.

I looked across the table at him and I could tell that this was just too much. Here it is that I had driven all these miles and he was there, so anxious to see me, only for us to spend an hour fussing about nothing. That is when I had a revelation. Never again would I use so much limited and precious time fussing and arguing. It was not worth it. Then to top it off to see the look on his face was more heartening than anything. I could tell that either I was getting on his nerves or that the fact that we were fussing at all was too much. Either way, that was not what I wanted to do. I don't like when things are tensed between us. It just feels so unnatural.

We believe in balance. Arguments create imbalance and where there is imbalance, there is trouble. We are supposed to be each other's peace. Every day he is in a place where he must keep up his defenses and stay on his toes. He deals with so much just being around other prisoners, dealing with correctional officers, and thinking about me and coming home. So, when visitation comes, that is not the time to create tension, but to create peace. It is a time to enjoy one another and just spend that quality time together. It is a time to take him out of that monotony that prison brings. I know that all married couples disagree and that all couples go through things. It is just a matter of getting through it without hurting or scaring the other. That is where our principles of marriage began to replay in my mind. It is one thing to talk the talk. Now it was time to walk the walk.

I decided to just shut up, bury the hatchet, and make sure that things between us were good. I understood that the focus is the care and concern of my husband. Nothing that was said at that moment would be more important than making sure that his heart was filled with my love and that his spirit was filled with peace. He is absolutely the same way. Besides, I was not going to see him again until the next weekend and I did not want his week to be plagued by what had happened during visitation. He has enough to go through without having to worry about a petty argument with me. So, I ended the argument, made up with my husband and enjoyed the rest of the visit.

I will say this though. I try to use every experience in my marriage as a lesson, no matter whether it is good or bad. Each day that you spend together is a chance to learn something that you did not know the day before. It is a day to correct wrong, learn from mistakes, love deeply, and to just keep building that strong foundation. Practice makes perfect and nothing beats a failure but a try. Who better to try with than someone that you are sharing your whole life with? Who better to grow with than someone who is looking to grow with you? My sweetheart is the ever so clever man, the perfect balance to me. He mellows me out, he calms my uneasiness, and he soothes my spirit. I can't help but to love him. We are alike in so many ways. However, it is our differences that provide such a balance. I can honestly and wholeheartedly say that my husband is the ying to my yang.

All in all, visitation is a good way to upkeep any type of relationship when the one you love is away. It gives you the chance to communicate and discuss things that a 15 minute phone call will not allow. It's the chance to see one another and to spend quality time with one another. Of course, it may not be that walk on the beach under the stars, or that picnic in the park, but the operative word is quality. I don't have to have all of those things to have quality time with my husband. Although I would love the chance to have those things with him, our situation does not allow us to. Therefore, we have to make the best of what we have been given. We are appreciative of that time, for visitation is a blessing. We both look forward to the day when this will no longer be our reality but at least with visitation, we can sit across from each other and prepare to manifest our visions into reality. To us, that is priceless.

Chapter 6

Common misconceptions of a prisoner's spouse

Only God can judge me is the common phrase used and heard around the world to describe a person's ability to judge another. So often, that is not the case. Many people feel as if it's their right to judge a person's character and try to inject their opinions or feelings into someone's life. The nerve of some people, huh? Why should my personal life be someone else's problem? At what point does the way that I conduct my life come up for open discussion? There is not a clear explanation as to why people do the things that they do or say the things that they say. But this is the world that we live in. People are often so quick to judge and assume when they have no right to. It is not fair but hey, this is life.

As the wife of an incarcerated man, I am often judged about many things ranging from why I decided to marry someone that was in prison to whether I am insane or not. I consider myself to be a strong-willed person but when I am asked those types of questions, I automatically jump to defense mode. It is not because I am intimidated or fear anyone but it is because I feel that I can make choices about my life on my own. I do not like being third-degreed about my decision to marry a man that is incarcerated. I am a grown and mature woman who can handle her life on her own. I should not have to defend my choice about who I want to marry or why I choose to stay with him. I do not or nor have I ever sought approval from anyone but God. If what I am doing is pleasing to Him then what the rest of the people in the world have to say simply does not matter to me.

Even with that, I am still asked the questions, still frowned upon, and still judged. While some questions can be valid and not meant to be disrespectful, there are some common misconceptions about a prisoner's wife. People have the tendency to assume things that they do not know. Now, while I do not claim to know everything, I know me and that is the only viewpoint that I can base this on. You will be surprised at some of the things that others think of us, wives and spouses but I am here to just set the record straight on a few things. Hopefully this will shed some insight on many of the misconceptions and judgments that are placed upon those like me, who have chosen to love someone that just so happens to be inside the walls.

Common Misconception #1. Prisoner's wives, spouses, and significant others have low self-esteem. Now I have a major problem with that. I wake up every morning and I look in the mirror and I smile. I do this not only because I am alive but I am beautiful as well. At the expense of sounding conceited, I happen to think that I am a very attractive woman. I am so cute, that I could kiss my damn self! I keep myself looking fabulous at all times. While I may not be a size two or have the shape of a model, I am comfortable with who I am and how I look. I love myself, inside and out. I love the woman that I have become, who I am, completely. I could not honestly take on the responsibility of the love, care, and concern of my husband if I did not first know how to love myself graciously. With that is accepting my own flaws and imperfections and embracing the makings of me. Yes, everyone has some things that they would like to change about their appearances but that's normal. Yes, we have been hurt or wronged but those things are what make you the strong person that you are. I love me, period.

I think highly of myself and that is because I know that regardless of what anyone says that I am beautiful. I am timeless, precious, and important. I am special, confident, and intelligent. I am a Queen, a mother, and a wife, full of love, beauty, and life. And those are things that I have embedded in my spirit and no one can take that away from me. When you have that knowledge and love of self, then that creates an environment for others to love or in some cases hate you as well. However, it starts within you.

Let's get this straight, my husband compliments me. He does not define me. I define who I am. My ways, integrity, actions, moral, and spiritual convictions define who I am. I am comfortable in my own skin and secure in the person that I am. I would and could be who I am whether I was with him or not. I am not with him out of desperation or despair. I do not feel devalued or worthless. In fact, it is very much the opposite. My husband makes me feel like I am just the most precious person in the world. He places me on this pedestal, high above anything. Coupled with the fact that I already am borderline conceited, I feel great about the woman that I am. I am with him because I love him and he loves me. I am in-love with a man who just happens to be in prison. Prison is merely his current location.

When I walk into a room, visitation or otherwise, my presence commands attention. It is not just because of *what I am wearing or how I look. It is because the beauty inside of me radiates from the inside out. So as you can see, there is no low self-esteem here. Besides, it should not matter what someone else thinks of you. The key word is "self"-esteem, the way that you feel about yourself. It is about embracing who you are and accepting the imperfections without hindrance. The opinion of another should not matter; at least that is how it works for me.*

Common Misconception #2. Prisoner's wives, spouses, and significant others are uneducated. In what rulebook, does it state that you must be illiterate to marry someone in prison? Where is it stated that you have to pass some kind of IQ to marry someone that is in prison? I have never heard of something sillier in my life. My choice to marry the man I love has nothing to do with whether I can read or write. Why do two people get married? They get married to make the ultimate commitment to one another. They get married to show that they are in love and dedicated to one another. There is no IQ test needed there. There is no education required to tell you that you love someone and want to marry them. So this misconception is definitely not a true one. Besides, I can both read and write. I can read and write so well that I have graduated from both high school and college with a diploma and two degrees, respectively. I hold a nursing certificate and am able to practice in any state that I go. I'm intelligent, witty, and as sharp as a tack. I am certified, qualified, and bonafide to love and live as I choose. I have chosen to marry the man that I love; not because I am uneducated but because I am smart enough to know with whom I want to spend the rest of my life with.

Common Misconception #3. Prisoner's wives, spouses, and significant others are lonely. Now wait a whole damn minute. There is a big difference between being alone and lonely. I learned that a very long time ago. First of all, if you are in a relationship with someone who is in prison, then you have to get used to being alone. The person that you love the most is not there with you. There is no one there to hold you in their arms at night or to kiss goodbye for work. I will admit that my husband goes above and beyond to fill the void that his lack of physical presence leaves. He has been succeeding at that very well. It is all what you make of it. It is all in the time and effort. Yes, holidays and birthdays are painful reminders of the love that's not with you. When people are going to couples only parties and events, you are alone, but that is only because of your current situation. Honestly, I have avoided the office and holiday parties where the spouses are there and that is because I do not want to be reminded of the fact that my husband is not here. But, that does not make me lonely; it makes me alone, temporarily alone.

I don't sit around in the dark hugging a pillow and crying my eyes out. I do what I need to do and make the best of my situation. Yes, there are days when I miss Zulu so bad that it hurts. I mean, the struggle is real. There are days when I crave his touch and the taste of his lips, simply because he is not physically here. I don't have that luxury right now. So, that makes me alone, not lonely. Every day that I am not with my husband is tough. Why wouldn't I be? That is my husband. I want him around me and he is not able to be here right now. There is nothing wrong with that. No one that I know would choose to be alone if not for a good reason. I have one. I am waiting on the release of my husband. As the old saying goes, the best things come to those who wait. Therefore, I am indeed waiting on the best, my Zulu is worth it. My love and devotion to him and only him is what governs and dictates my actions in our marriage.

Common Misconception #4. Prisoner's wives, spouses, and significant others have absolutely nothing to do besides sit in the house and wait on phone calls. Wow, there is something that I clearly can't agree with. There is more to life than just sitting and waiting on telephone calls. Although your spouse is incarcerated, you are not and time waits for no one. I think that it is important that any spouse gets out and experience life other than just that of marriage, kids, and work. Granted, your spouse is not there but the life still has to go on. It is okay to go out and spend some time to just take care of yourself. Everyone deserves some time for just themselves, whether it's a night out with the girls or just crawling into bed with a good book. Having some "pamper me" time allows you the chance to relax, re-energize, and rejuvenate. One thing that I do know is that when you feel better about yourself, then everything that you do will be a reflection of that feeling.

If you are like me, then you cannot afford to just sit and wait on phone calls. You have to work. You have duties that you have to attend to. There are the children that have to be provided for, bills, and responsibilities. We are preparing for life beyond his incarceration. We are constantly and consistently building our foundation. The plan is not for us to spend the rest of our lives working for someone else. We are building our own brand, setting up *our own businesses, and that takes a substantial amount of work. Not to mention, there is the fact that you have to pay for those calls that others claim that you sit and wait on. Trust me when I tell you, nothing about prison is cheap. My drive to visitation alone is a little costly. Now don't get me wrong, I love talking to my husband as often as I can and I will talk to him as much as I can afford to. However, I can't just stop living and stay by the phone. You must continue on living and being productive. I am sure that your loved one would not be pleased with you sitting and withering away. They live through you and you have to live for you. They depend on you to be strong and to hold the fort down while they are away. My husband has a winner in his wife and I refuse to sit and become stagnant in my actions or in my thinking. When I wake up, I'm moving and working towards securing and solidifying our future. Once he calls, I will undoubtedly stop and talk to him but I will never stop working. The grind never stops.*

Common Misconception #5. Marriages where one spouse is in prison almost always end in divorce. What can I say about this one? I am not lost on the fact that there are a number of marriages that end in divorce. But, that fact includes marriages in general and it does not specify marriages of prisoners. Divorce is a true reality. There are some people who choose to end their marriages due to whatever their personal or mutual reasons are. Although I am a hopeless romantic, I am not clueless to the fact that marriage takes a lot of work to survive. Sustaining a marriage in prison is no different than any other marriage. The only thing that differentiates it is the fact that one of the spouses is in prison and there is the lack of physical presence. That is just geography, only location. Every marriage experiences trials and tribulations. We all have fussed, argued, screamed, yelled, and been angry at our spouses at some point. What matters is how you handle that and what you do going forward. How you handle the trying times is what builds and strengthens your relationship. Marriage is a constant learning experience.

I look at the marriages of my aunt and grandparents and I find myself amazed. They have been married for years; I am talking decades together. I am sure that they have been through many things, however, they continue to love, forgive, trust, and fight for their marriage. See, many times I see marriages fail because no one is willing to admit fault or guilt. Asking for forgiveness or granting forgiveness is viewed as a sign of weakness or naivety. Spouses tend to get stuck in their egos and let pride get in the way of really saying the things that they are feeling or needing to be understood. They hold each other's faults against them and are not willing to let go of the past and move on. How can you expect to move into the future if you keep living in the past? The truth is that people can sabotage their own happiness by so many things. Marriage is what you make of it. It takes work, dedication, and time. You must nurture it, protect it, and feed it. Without change, there is no growth and without growth there is the possibility of death. Divorce is a matrimonial death. It is up to you to breathe life into or accept death in your marriage.

If we want to continue to thrive, then we must be willing to learn and grow. Marriage is what you make of it. If you build it on a solid foundation, then no storm will be able to knock it down. Whoever said that a marriage can't

last, just ask my grandparents who have been together for
50 years or my aunt and uncle who had been together for
over 30 years. The fact that my husband is in prison only
means that we are not physically together all the time. We
still have the same issues, the same worries, cares, and
concerns as other people who are married and living
together on the outside. His current residential status
doesn't mean anything. We are happily married. However,
that has not come without incident. It has taken work to
get to the place that we are now. It has been a journey but
when you have someone who is willing and ready to go the
distance, then it makes things so much easier.

    Before Zulu and I got married, we decided that
divorce is not an option. We took that completely out of our
life's equation. With divorce not being an option, it meant
that we were both going to have to really work on our
marriage. We both desire the types of marriage that our
older loved ones have. We know that takes a lot of work but
we are willing to do that because we love one another. The
fact that we are not physically together does place a tiny
hurdle on our marriage, but it is nothing that we cannot
handle. We just get creative and spend as much time
together as we possibly can. We communicate whether it is
by phone, email, letters, or visitation. I told Zulu at the start
of this relationship that the same things that we did in the
beginning of our relationship are not going to be enough to
sustain our marriage. And why you may ask? That is
because anything that you want to thrive has to grow.
Things change constantly and consistently. For instance, if
you want a plant to grow, you have to water it, sit in the
sunlight, and take care of it. Eventually that plant is going

to grow and grow bigger than the pot that it was originally in. If you don't move your thriving plant to a bigger pot, then eventually it is going to start falling to pieces and eventually wither away and die.

Common Misconception #6. Prisoner's spouses are only good for visits, conversations, and commissary. Now this is chuckling to me. There are some men who do sit back and prey on the needs and insecurities of others to get what they want. I have seen it happen so many times. But, it is all part of getting to know the person that you are dealing with. The problem is that people jump into these things and get so wrapped up in their perception of a person, rather than taking the time to get to know who they truly are. Anyone can tell you something that you want to hear. Anyone can finesse you and have you thinking one thing and it is totally the opposite. Actions speak louder than words and trust me; a person's true intentions will reveal themselves. You just have to be receptive to hearing and seeing it. It is only so long that a person can hold up on some crap, for what is done in the dark will surely come to light. Remember, when someone shows you who they are the first time, believe it.

If they are anything like my husband, you will know that all men are not leeches or game runners. There are men who believe that they are supposed to take care of themselves and provide for their wives and children. Incarceration does hinder that but the premise is still the same. My husband does not ask me for anything. He does not demand that I send him money or buy him trivial materialistic things. He does not try to sell me dreams and rainbows to get the things that he wants or needs. My *husband looks to do the opposite. He does whatever he can to lighten my worries and not contribute to them. He believes in a man working and providing for his wife and children. His current situation just does not allow him to do so. Although my husband is incarcerated, he has morals and values and the mistake that he made to land him in prison was not a result of him being raised immorally. Now don't get me wrong, I love visiting with, talking to, and knowing that my husband can have the things that he needs. But that is not the basis of our relationship.*

Common Misconception #7. The life of a prisoner's spouse is for those that are weak. Wow! Some of the things that I have heard are just plain ridiculous. This life is not for the weak and easily broken. This life is not for one who is uncomfortable with being alone or are unable to adapt to change. It takes a strong person to withstand and endure all the things that come with being the spouse of a prisoner. Prison life is all about swift change and uncertainty. Lockdowns, riots, transfers, and segregation, all occur suddenly and often without notice. There have been times when I was not able to visit Zulu or talk to him for as much as 21 days. Imagine it being almost a month, not knowing what is going on with your better half. Imagine what it is like to not know if they are hurt, tired or hungry. Imagine what it is like to look at the news and see an incident that occurred at your spouse's prison and not know if he was in some way affected by it. Imagine craving their touch or just wanting to feel some kind of relief that can only be achieved by the sound of their voice. You can't begin to imagine how hard those things are.

To the average person, dealing with prison life would be hard. Damn, it is hard. It can be frustrating, irritating, and unnerving. However, it can also be a loving, blissful, wonderful experience. Yes, I said that. Because if you love someone, you don't allow the limitations to dictate how you feel. You do not let those things keep you from achieving and obtaining the happiness that is within and loving the person that you are with. It is all what you make of it. It is all about what you put into it. Just as with anything, the high moments are wonderful. But, if you can't handle the low moments of this life then this life is just not for you. I know women who have not been able to touch or kiss their spouses in years because of the various segregation programs. They have to see their spouses through glass. I can't even fathom not being able to touch my husband's face or kiss his lips. I crave those things after one week so I can only imagine how the others must feel not being able to do that for months and sometimes even years. Dealing with uncertainty and having to adjust to swift change is enormous. Not to mention, dealing with a person who has so many inner emotions and feelings and are in a place where they are not really able to express them. The insurmountable amount of strength that this takes is incredible. So, no, this life is not for the weak and easily broken. It takes strength and endurance to run this race. It takes determination and will-power. But most of all, it takes love.

These are just some of the common misconceptions that I have heard when it comes to prisoner's wives, spouses, and significant others. In a world full of imperfect people, it is important that we try to understand one another. If there is no chance of understanding, there should at least be respectful of the choices that people make. We are all imperfect and because we are, we have no right to judge others because of the choices that they make. Karma is real. The ultimate judgement is that of the Most High.

Throughout this whole ordeal, I have learned that there is no discrimination on love. When you love someone and I mean truly love someone, there is no imperfection that you can't set aside, there is no location barrier, and there is no judgment. If we all learned to love one another and learned to respect one another's decisions, then the world would be a better place. We need to learn to be supportive of one another instead of tearing each other down. How are we ever supposed to rise to our fullest potential when we are constantly seeking to destroy one another? It takes too much energy to hate and judge. People are going to do what they want, when they want, and how they want until they themselves decide on something different. Who are we to judge?

As a prisoner's wife, I often have to defend my relationship with my husband to those who choose to be judgmental. That is something that I do not mind doing. Although, I shouldn't have to, I have no problem putting someone in their place or answering a valid question about my marriage. My marriage is a sense of pride, a badge of honor. It was founded by the same principles that any other marriage was founded on. Don't let the location fool you. Prison doesn't dictate my marriage and how I feel about my husband. Some people do not understand why it is that I choose to stand by my husband. But again, it is my choice. If you don't understand something, ask questions, do research, and just don't judge me or others who choose to stand by the ones that we love. You would be surprised at how the lives of a prisoner's spouse are not too much more complicated than the lives of the free spouses. Some people may not like my choices. Others may call names and become critical. Everyone has their opinion and as I said before, I do not live my life to seek the approval of anyone other than God. So even if you don't agree, kindly respect the choices that I have made for my life.

Chapter 7

Sex and Intimacy

One of the most special things about a relationship is the sex and intimacy. As the wife of a prisoner, I am often asked how my husband and I keep the sex and intimacy part of our relationship alive with him being in prison. Whenever I hear such a question, I am taken aback just a little. It seems to be a rather personal question but I can understand the curiosity of some people. Some people are actually wondering how it is. Others are looking for tips and advice. And then you have some people who are just being plain nosey. Regardless of the reason, I answer. I am not ashamed at all. So, after I have gotten over the initial feeling of shock, I chuckle. The reason is because Zulu and I get very creative when it comes to sex and intimacy. He is incarcerated so it's not a matter of just jumping in the bed and making the headboard squeak. Creativity is in full effect. My husband and I have become quite the connoisseurs when it comes to that. Now, allow me to elaborate.

We happen to live in states do not allow conjugal visits or trailer visitations or any of the sorts. Believe me when I tell you, it really unnerves me. I even get a little envious of the other few states that allow them. I look at the reality TV shows that showcase the stories of prison wives and I sit there wishing like hell that I could have some of the same privileges. There was one lady that was packing up food and clothes and getting ready for a trailer visit with her husband. She was able to spend the entire *weekend with him alone. They got the chance to cook, live together, and just have quality time together. Honestly, I would love to have the chance to spend 42 hours alone with my husband. That would be a non-stop sexcapade for real. I would let him up so we could eat, talk, and take a shower but best believe we would definitely be getting it in. I mean, who wouldn't? I am mad that we are not afforded the chance to have "family visits". There are only a very few states that have them. It is a shame that more states don't have them. I know that a lot of problems would be solved if they could release some of that pinned up sexual tension.*

According to some research that I have done, conjugal visits have reduced the violence in prison, recidivism rates, and even the occurrence of incidences of sexual violence in prison. The reason for trailer and family visits are not just for the sex and intimacy, but to also get the chance to just have some normal, quality private time. It is the chance to connect and interact with family. Those types of visits seem to provide some sense of normalcy that you don't have every day. It gives you a chance to bond and to really get the chance to experience what it is like to live with another person. Yes, the visits are only for a few days but you will be surprised as to how much you learn about a person by living with them. There is one thing to the phone calls, letters, and visits but it is a whole other ordeal to have to live with someone. Living with someone is a big step. There is so much that you have to learn about that person's way of living. And there has to be some compatibility and compromise in order for it to work both inside and outside of the prison walls. So these types of visits can shed some insight as to what life will be like when they are released.

Too bad, Georgia does not afford that opportunity. There is still hope though. It's a slim hope but still hope.

There are different ways to keep your love life spicy and sexually satisfying while your sweetheart is in prison. The best part is that these ways do not involve cheating. It is purely based on sexual stimulation and creativity. There are dreams, letters, pictures, and of course phone sex. The trick is that you have to become creative. You and your sweetie have to really discuss what the two of you like and get into details about what turns you on. Find out what makes you feel good and use those things to your advantage. Sex and intimacy is a chance to explore the sensual and intimate side of the two of you.

When my husband and I first got together, we would write letters about all the things that we want to do with and for one another. I would have these erotic dreams and fantasies. They were filled with hot, wild, and passionate sex. I would have dreams about us getting it on in the park, or in the car, or while standing the rain. I am talking about dreams that were so hot that I felt like I needed to smoke a cigarette afterwards. I would wake up soaked in my own juices, panties wet and all. That's how hot they were. As soon as I would wake up and dry off, I would find myself rushing to a pen and paper just to write about my dream. I would go into details, down to every touch, kiss, suck, moan, and groan. I described everything from the sensation of his tongue down my spine to the exact moment that I climaxed. Then I would seal it with the scent of my perfume and mail it to my honey.

Writing a letter with that much intensity was so fun. The more intense I got, the more he enjoyed it. I could bring him into my fantasy and allow him to see how much passion and desire that I had for him. He would then take what I had just written and go even further, sending that letter back to me for me to continue on with the fantasy. It was great and very satisfying. We both got so much pleasure out of that and for a little while, our fantasy letters would quench that sexual appetite that was inside of us.

After a while of our sensual letter writing, we decided to up the fun up a notch. It's one thing to read a letter but to see the sexual suggestions was something completely different. It made the letters stand out even more. Now the Department of Corrections is very strict as to what you can send into the facilities when it comes to sexual suggestive pictures. So, I would make sure that I was completely covered but made sure that I posed in a provocative manner. That way, I was obeying the rules while giving my husband the thrill that he desired. My husband got so many pictures of me that he had to get two photo albums. I remember taking a picture sucking on a lollipop, or flicking out my tongue which shows my tongue ring, and perfectly glossed lips. I did the "eating the banana" shot, posing in a way that would awaken the dead and everything. It was a turn on to me and an even bigger turn on for him.

Keeping in mind that sex is about a combination of the stimulating of the senses, it was now time advance to the next level. Now that he had his readable and visual things, it was time to take it up another notch and add the sound effects. This is where the phone sex came into play. Not many people are comfortable with having phone sex *but it is a great way to explore that sensual side of one another. Yes, the phone calls are recorded and that can give you a feeling of hesitancy but I am sure that a correctional officer would rather hear the sounds and thoughts of sex than to hear of something illegal and potentially dangerous to the safety and security of the institution. Phone sex is legal, fun, and if done right, it can be a pleasurable experience. Stimulating his senses and creating a mood that is conducive to love making. I love the fact that I can take him away from that place and bring him in even closer to me.*

These are the things that lead up to phone sex and that is great. Just know that if your phone sex is spicy, that can lead to masturbation. Yes, I said it. We know that prisons try to discourage sexual exploration and masturbation but you have to remember that in a state that does not allow conjugal visits, this is all that they have. And although he may not be able to do it himself, he can damn sure have a good time imagining me doing it. Understand that human sexuality is a part of life no matter where you are or who you are. It is something that I am not ashamed of at all. And it is my opinion that so many people are much happier and easier to get along with after they have unleashed that sexual tension. I know that I am. I don't see anything wrong with it if it is done in a respectful way and in your own private space. I am at home and this man is my husband, so I don't see anything wrong with that.

I have an imagination that is out of this world so I always manage to come up with something. I find ways to make things interesting. I have my cell phone and there have been times that my husband and I have had phone sex in the car. I pull up in my back yard, turn on the radio, cover myself with my jacket, and have a good time listening to the sound of my husband's voice. The change of scenery is exciting. Just as I said earlier, you have to stimulate the senses. If my husband closes his eyes, he can imagine what we would actually be doing in a car if he was here with me. I create the ambiance and we capitalize on the experience. We capitalize on the opportunity.

Sex is not the only aspect to a healthy relationship. There is also the intimacy. The degree of intimacy is extremely limited since most prisons do not allow excessive amounts of touching or displays of affection. I make sure that we make the most out of the moments that we are given. At the prison where he is located, you have the opportunity to kiss and embrace at the beginning and at the end of the visit. We have to sit across from one another and we are not allowed to hold hands at all. Intimacy in this case can seem rather impossible but just as I said before, we take whatever opportunity that we are given and we make the best of it. You better know we are going to sneak some kisses in when we can.

When I enter the visitation room, the opportunity begins. My husband walks up to me and that's when I softly grab his face and kiss him passionately. Now, we are sure to keep in mind that there are often children present and that the guards are watching so we do it in a way that is not offensive to anyone. It is at that time, that he will hold my hand and look deeply into my eyes. And for a second, everyone disappears and it's just him and I standing there. It's a beautiful moment. It is moments like those that make *all of this worth it. You forget that they damn near stripped searched you, that you had to get undressed, and all that just to get to experience that moment.*

During the visit, we look for the chance to steal a kiss or hold hands. I love when my hubby opens his hand and extends it towards me. Whenever he says that, I already know what he is about to do. He rubs my legs, caresses my arms, and looks at me as if he can see deeply into my soul. I place my hands gently on his face and just feel the smile on his face. In a place where he has nothing to smile about, I can, for that brief moment, take him away with me. Whenever we are that affectionate, it is an overwhelming feeling of love. I look in his eyes and I see everything that I could ever want or need in him. I lose myself in his beautiful eyes and this warm feeling takes over me. At that moment, it's not about sex; it's not about masturbation or climaxing. That is the feeling of love. It is intimacy.

The end of visitation is such an incredible time for us. I usually stay until the end of visitation for the day because that is when we have the chance to really enjoy our good-byes. Those extra few minutes can make your whole week right. At this time, there is a major crowd of people. Everyone is standing up, hugging, kissing, and embracing. Subsequently, there is not a lot of direct watching. So, there is another opportunity to sneak in some "sweet time" with my husband. I have to be careful because he is just so greedy. Once I let him do something, he just can't get enough. I mean, can you blame him? My husband has a gorgeous, sexy wife. I mean, I am 5 foot 6 inches of soft caramel lusciousness and I am all his. Shoot, he knows what's good.

Some people may argue that there is nothing like the real thing. Okay, point taken. I have heard people say so many times that you need to have the real thing to keep from being frustrated and agitated. To me, that is just an excuse to cheat. Sex is sex whether its phone or masturbation. So, um yeah, I am going to need to hear a better excuse. No, phone sex and masturbation is not the same as the real physical contact. But again, this situation is not like others. Your spouse is incarcerated and there must never be any cheating. I don't care what type of relationship, agreement, or arrangement that you have. Having sex with someone other than your spouse is cheating. I am not about that life at all. My body is reserved for only my husband. So, if I can't have sex with him, then I will have sex with my damn self! I am not about to do something that I know is wrong for the sake of some quick pleasure. To take the risk losing the respect and trust of my husband is not worth it. To have to look at yourself in the mirror knowing that you have went against your vows? It's clearly not worth it. What would I look like?

Here it is we are living in a world where sex is wild and devalued. People are running around sleeping with other people, on the down low, and everything else. They aren't disclosing anything and keeping everything hidden. The AIDS, HIV, Syphilis, and Herpes rates are out of this word, and you want to take the risk of catching something? Hell no! Not me. I can and will wait on my husband. I am not taking a gamble like that. There is no sex in the world worth that much. So yes, I can just handle that with my husband in our own way until he gets home. Because trust me, when I finally get to lay it on his ass the way I want to, it's a wrap. So, while he is in there working out, getting that back right, I am going to stay faithful and keep these walls tight.

After all is said and done, sex and intimacy is not impossible just because your sweetheart is in prison. You and your loved one just have to be comfortable with one another explore that sensuous side. Creativity and imagination is the key to achieving sexual pleasure and quenching that sexual desire that burn within. While nothing can take the place of actually making love, appealing to and stimulating the senses can only serve to enhance and improve your relationship. Just imagine how all this preparation and waiting is going to magnify your attraction to one another. All of this will just build up the anticipation for the day that they come home and you really get to just be freaky. Everything that you both have been talking about and dreaming about will finally go down. Imagine the fireworks that are going to go off that day, and I am not even talking about the 4th of July.

We constantly find ways to bring excitement to our limited sex life but I promise you that if you take the time to get creative, it will be a wonderful part of your relationship. If you choose or refuse to indulge in your sexual creativity, the sex and intimacy between the both of you will become boring and dull. Then after a while, it will seem more like a chore than a pleasurable experience. Invest in a sex toy or a massager. Stock up on batteries. Talk as freaky as you want and foster the fantasy. Play games that will allow you and your sweetheart to explore *the sensual side of the both of you. Toss those inhibitions to the side and allow your imagination to run wild and free. Step outside that safe place and just allow yourself to be free to explore that wild and sensual side. What better person to be more uninhibited with than your spouse?*

Of course, it is natural to feel some type of apprehension but after you toss that aside and become more comfortable, it is really something that you will grow to enjoy. You have to understand that everyone has a sexual appetite and it needs to be fed. Just because you are incarcerated does not mean that you no longer have those urges. You just have to get more creative as to how you feed them. It has taken a lot of communication, exploration, and understanding for us to get to this point. Now that we have, we have been able to create and maintain the limited sexual and intimate side of our relationship. It works for my husband and me. Besides, what a better way to spend some time with the person that you love? Just think, if he can turn me on by the sound of his voice, imagine what it's going to be like when I get it all. I'm hype!

Chapter 8

Truth, Trust & Honesty

How wonderful would it be if everyone was honest and truthful? I can't tell you how many times I have heard "Keep it real" or "I keep it 100". If I had a dollar for every time I heard those words, I would be rich. People often spew those sayings but barely live up to what they truly mean or what is politically correct about them. Wouldn't it be incredible if people would mind their own business and tend to their own affairs? Sadly, we don't live in that type of world. We live in a world in which people feel that it is better to drag you down rather than lift you up. We live in a world in which people that claim to love you are the same ones who are secretly waiting for your downfall just to say "I told you so". We live in a world in which the fantasy of a lie outweighs the realness of the truth. Now how does that fit into my life?

When a person is incarcerated, people often adopt the "out of sight, out of mind" notion. Some also adopt the "what he doesn't know won't hurt him" frame of mind. That is not the case with me. I think that truth, trust, and honesty are important in any relationship, especially when a spouse is in prison. The level of commitment to my husband is high. I feel as if adopting and implementing those character traits are essential in a relationship no matter what the circumstance is. I am always sure to conduct myself in the same way that I would if my husband was right here. I honor myself as a woman and respect my husband and our marriage. There is no wavering or *hesitating in that at all. I am not about to go out here and cheapen my value as a woman. I am a Queen and if I want that respect, then I must conduct myself in that manner. I am convicted by my morals, guided by my conscience, and true to the vows that I have taken with this man. What people fail to realize is that honesty is not just reserved for the things that we can see. Honesty builds the foundation of trust for the things that we can't see.*

It takes a mountain of faith and love to cast down the spirits of doubt. One would have to be really secure in their relationship in order to push those thoughts aside and continue to trust and have faith in their loved one and in the relationship. My husband and I make every conscience effort to be truthful in our relationship. I am proud to say that we do a damn good job at that. Not only is he my husband, but he is also my better half, my best friend. There is nothing that should be off limits to me and vice versa. We are always supposed to be honest and truthful with one another, no matter what. Sometimes, the truth is not always pleasant but I would rather for him to give me the ugly truth than to spoil me with a beautiful lie. Keeping things open and honest ensures that we maintain a strong, healthy, and meaningful relationship. Trust is precious. It is so easy to earn but once you destroy it, it is so much harder to gain back.

Sometimes, there are occurrences that happen and then there are other people who see it necessary to intrude their thoughts and opinions about a relationship. My husband and I have experienced this several times during the course of our marriage. The thing of it is that you have to be secure in your relationship and have that trust and honesty in order to stand against the troubles that can come against you. People are often envious of what they don't have. When they see people who are in-love and happy, they tend to want to break that up and set out to destroy your relationship. We live in the "side piece" age, where people think that it is okay to share. They find pleasure in going into other people's relationships with the intent to cause drama or to break them up. We live in the time where a wedding ring is not a deterrent but an invitation. People have lost respect for the sanctity of marriage and constantly disrespect the sacredness of relationships. Because of this, the premise of trust has been jaded, shaded, and in some cases, even broken. Knowing that, it is even more important that a marriage is built strongly on that foundation of truth, trust, and honesty.

One of my rules of thumb, if you have to sneak, hide, deny, or lie about it, then you should not be doing it. If you wouldn't do it while your spouse was standing there, then you should not be doing it when he is not. People tend to foolishly believe that people in prison don't find out things. On that same respect, incarcerated spouses should also not be foolish enough to believe that they can do things without their free spouses finding out as well. People tend to think that just because our incarcerated loved ones are secluded from the rest of the world, that they don't have any connection with it. That could be further from the truth. People that are incarcerated find out things just as fast as we on the outside do and sometimes even before we do. I have never been foolish to believe that my husband could not find out any information that he wanted to find out if he wanted to just as he could never be foolish enough to believe that I could not find out anything that I needed to know. But fear that he would find out is not a reason to be truthful. It is a pitiful excuse. My reason is because I love this man and I am convicted my morals and bonded by the covenant of my marriage. I stood before God and this man and said that I love, honor, and cherish him; that I would "Keep unto him and only him". This man trusts me with the very beat of his heart and when I stood before him and told him that there would be him and only him, I sure as hell meant it.

You have to always remember to conduct yourselves with the highest of integrity and respect at all times. Yes, temptation is real and that is understandable being that your spouse is not able to physically be with you. At this test of wills, you are going to have to decide if one moment of weakness is worth a lifetime of pain. You have to choose if that one moment is worth losing the trust and respect of the person that you love the most. Yes, there is the possibility of forgiveness. They may say that they forgive you and they understand but trust me, they may forgive but they don't forget. Yes, they may accept it and say that it is okay but understand that cloud of doubt will remain there until they are able to truly forgive and to heal. It is just not worth the risk. Who would purposely want to live life under a cloud of disloyalty and distrust? Trust is so easy to give but when you destroy it, it is hard as hell to get back.

Understand now, this trust, truth, and honesty thing is not one sided. I expect my husband to act the same way and conduct himself in a way that is conducive to the goals what we have set in our marriage. I trust him to honor his vows to me as well. I expect him to be honest with and to be forthcoming with me. I expect him to be truthful and to trust me as well. This goes both ways. You always have to be willing to get as good as you give. You cannot demand something of someone that you are not willing to do yourself. Relationships and marriage are not one sided. It takes the time, effort, and love of two people to make it work. Just like with anything, there will be times that you are tested. It is at those times when you must exercise your faith in one another and in your relationship.

I will say this. Karma is real. See people don't understand that you can't walk around doing wrong and hurting people and then expecting something good to happen for you. Yes, you may think that you can get away with something but trust and believe, you will reap what you sow. There will be something will happen to make you recognize the error of your ways. Another thing to know is that you will not be blessed for breaking your vows and going outside of your marriage, and neither will the other person. I have witnessed that before. When a person decides to go against their covenant and break the marital bond, God will make you pay for that. Word of caution, stay out of people's relationships and marriages and do not allow anyone to interfere with yours.

The love and level of commitment that we have for one another surpasses any fence, any gate, any shakedown or any guard. I trust in him as he does in me. I believe in him, his morals, and his commitment to me, and the principles that we stand on. Truth, trust, honesty, and loyalty all go hand in hand. You cannot have a relationship with one and not the others. It just won't work. Zulu and I are the creators of our inner universe. Anything and everything that happens within it is a direct result of what we put into it. A woman will always feel protected by her man if she feels that she can trust him. In return, a man will always protect and defend his woman when he feels that he can trust her.

Physical separation and limitations can yield to difficulties in trust when a person is incarcerated. It is up to me to make sure that my spouse is comfortable and secure with us. It is up to me to make sure that he feels secure and trusting with me. It means conducting myself with respect and integrity in my ways and actions, and considering his thoughts and feelings in everything that I do. It means being the righteous woman that he married, the one that he chose to give his last name. I am bonded by my word, bonded in my covenant to him. I demand that same respect and loyalty from him as well. There will be tests and trials but if we are honest and forthcoming with one another, then there is nothing that we can't get through. Loyalty and trust is a must in any relationship.

My Hubby and I were matching!

Chapter 9

Choices

When I was younger I was constantly lectured about choices and consequences. I have even done a lot of living and learning. I have come to find, that in life, everyone has a choice. With those choices are consequences. While some may be good and others are bad, there are consequences nonetheless. The choices that we make will have consequences that will affect us for the rest of our lives. In some way, they are going to shape our relationships, our jobs, our education, and our futures. It will dictate our earning potential, our thinking, our feelings, and our views and perceptions. They affect us even well after it has all happened, even affecting those that we love and care about.

When my husband was younger, he made a choice to get himself entangled with the wrong crowd and begin doing things that were not necessarily morally and legally correct. As a result of this choice, he ended up going to prison and having to spend a considerable amount of his life in there. As a result, he left family that cares about him and a chance to live the life that he wanted. He deprived himself of the opportunity to live by his own means, under his own terms and at his highest potential. Because of his choice, he has been subjected to persecution, judgment, solitude, and confinement. While these things are the direct consequences of the choice that he made, it has served as a learning experience and given him time to truly reflect on his life and his true purpose. See, sometimes we get so *caught up in the moment, doing what we feel is right, or doing what we want that we forget that with every action, there is a reaction. With every choice that we make, there is a consequence that will to be addressed.*

I applaud my husband and some of the people whom I have gotten the chance to meet during this journey. Some of these guys have not allowed their circumstances to dictate who and what they choose to do with their time. It is easy to get caught up in the prison politics, gangs, and foolishness that can come along with prison life. But, the guys that I have interacted with have been dedicated to improving their lives and making their time count for something. They want to come home and take their rightful place in society. It is their wish to take care of their families and become the productive citizens that they should have been from the beginning.

Some people, my husband included, have made the choice to turn their lives around seeking rehabilitation and yearning for the chance to make amends for the wrongs of their pasts. I can't tell you how delighted I am with the purposeful change that my husband has made in his life. I know his struggle. I have seen and heard his pain and sadness. It would be so easy for him to succumb to the pain of his past, to the despair that is constantly around him. However, he has endured this with great fortitude and I am just overwhelmed by the amount of strength that he possesses to do that. I am overjoyed with how he has overcome the insurmountable odds and has pushed himself into his true purpose by seeking knowledge and restructuring his character into something that both his wife and children can be proud of. I am overjoyed that he has grown to be consciously aware of himself and the path in life that he was destined to take. The journey to self-discovery is not an easy one but is necessary in order to be able to proceed on the path to righteousness and integrity.

Spirituality and religion have often played part in a person's choice to better themselves. The need of that spiritual being or spiritual level of enlightenment has proven to be beneficial to those that are behind the walls. They help with creating positive and inspirational relationships both inside and outside of the prison walls. These are choices that these individuals have made. Although it may have taken a drastic occurrence such as confinement and prison, religion and spirituality are still wonderful things to partake in. Regardless of the specific religious or spiritual guidance, any religion or spiritual journey that promotes unity, growth, and positivity is good choice. Religions and spirituality fosters growth, responsibility, and personal accountability. It also teaches patience and awareness. These traits are helpful and integral in the shaping of the mind and spirit.

Now, I believe in conviction and accountability. I believe that when you do something that offends, hurts, or harms someone that you should be held responsible and accountable for it. If circumstances warrant it, you also should be punished for your actions. All of that has to deal the choices that we make and the consequences that we will receive as a result of those choices. Yes, I believe that there should be a level of degree but nevertheless, there has to be some consequence given. Consequences serve as learning tools. It gives us a chance to reflect back on the decisions of life and to guide you into making choices that will be both beneficial and conducive to your growth and development.

When you interact with someone who is in prison, so many things go through your mind. There are so many thoughts, so many questions. You wonder what they did to get themselves in prison. You ask if they have remorse or feel any shame or guilt about what they have done. You wonder why they did it and why they didn't make a different choice. So much goes through your mind. I do not believe that everyone who is in prison is a bad person. There are some people who are the victim of circumstance, casualties in the war of life. Please understand that you do have some people who are just pure evil, but others that are there who truly want to atone for the wrong choice that they have made and want to correct themselves.

Although there are people who have made bad choices and have done evil things, I believe that they should not be void of love. Love is a universal emotion. It is not just reserved for certain things, people, and places. Even the most prolific serial killers are loved by someone. They may even have loved someone themselves. They have just made terrible choices that have deemed them as being evil and unable to be rehabilitated. In some instances, that may be actually so. But because they have chosen to do such horrific things, they are suffering the major consequences of their choices. And in many cases, they are being left alone to suffer for the crime that they have committed. Nevertheless, they have left families and loved ones behind who are affected by their incarceration just as much as the offender.

This experience has taught me so much about choices. It has made me understand that you are truly responsible for the choices that you make. Prison is more than the little scenes from the made-for-TV movies. It is a real place where real things happen. Some of those things are good and other things are bad. There are real people in prison. These people are angry, depressed, and sad. Some are harsh, mean, and brutal. Some wish to rehabilitate while others are just there to do their time and get out. There are even some people with no regard to human life or without conscience. Ultimately the choices that have made which brought them to prison and what they do while they are there will determine what they do once they come home. By then, the choice is up to them to get out and be productive or to be counterproductive and fall back into recidivism.

Watching my husband in prison is tough. Knowing the struggle that he goes through every day is hard for me to hear, hard for me to even imagine. I remember the day that he got transferred and all I could think of was the fact that he was going to be chained and handcuffed. The thought alone was enough to rip my heart into shreds. He sees and endures a lot, mostly having to deal with the fact that he has left his family out here without him, knowing that they truly need him. He longs for the life that he could have had if he were not in there. He has missed so such of his life because he has had to spend it in prison. He is now married and has a wife and children who are ready and waiting for him to come home. It is really difficult for him and for many others. Now, I know that prison life is not easy and in no way should it be but there should always be some humanity there. However, all the issues that he is experiencing are because of a choice that he made. And just as I have always said, there are consequences to the choices that we make whether it is good or bad.

My hope for so many is that those that are incarcerated take the experience of prison use it to turn their lives around. I hope that they take this time and really think about the consequences of their actions. I want them to think about how the choices that they have made have affected their victims, victims' families, as well as their own families. There are so many spouses left without out here alone. Children are growing up without their parents. Mothers and fathers are aching for their children. Incarceration does not just affect the person that committed the crime. It also affects others.

I hope that those who are incarcerated share their experiences with their children and others to teach them that prison is not what they want to have to experience. So many times, I listen to rap music and jail, drugs, and crime is so glorified. What the rap music does not tell is the stories of the people that have to endure the pain and suffering of it. The rap music does not tell that there are mothers who pass out in the courtroom after the judge and jury has convicted their son or daughter. What they do not tell about is the tears that roll down the faces of children as they watch their parents being taken out in handcuffs. They do not rap about the spouses that are left out to struggle and raise children all on their own. Rap music doesn't describe the enormous emptiness that I feel when I have to leave my husband there. It doesn't talk about how I have to bite down on my bottom lip just to keep from crying. Don't *get me wrong, I do not have anything against rap music, but we have to all learn that there is a difference between the truth of one and the fantasy of another. Yes, some rap is based on the real lives and struggles of others but we have to use rap as a message and not as a blueprint on how to live.*

We have to learn and teach our children that prison is real and it is not a place that they want to end up. Life is too short to make mistakes that will take time away from it. I know that my husband has spent too long in prison and our children suffer because of that. They have missed so much and so has he. Sometimes, we as parents think that the things that we do don't bother our children but as a mother, I constantly see the affect that Zulu's incarceration has on our kids. It is a terrible lesson that they had to learn but we have an example of what consequence that making bad choices can have. One of the positives that will come out of this situation is that he will be coming home soon. Our children will have time to spend with their father and he will have the chance to be the father that they need.

I am not lost on the fact that there are some who will spend the rest of their lives in prison. I pray that they find peace and strength to endure it. I pray that their loved ones will have the same. Just know that a life sentence does not mean that you can't be productive or that life has no meaning. You still have the choice to make your life meaningful and leave a legacy that will not just highlight your crime. You can still be educated, still be a respectable person, and to still live a productive life. Your life will always mean something and each day that you are given is a chance to live it as best as possible. You still have the chance to teach others and to share your past mistakes and wisdom with others. You are not forgotten and you are not alone. There are people who love and care about you. So make the choice to live as wonderfully as you can. We all must make our lives count for something for if you die without ever living, then you were living in vain.

Life is all about choices. We all have them. Just know and understand that with every choice that you make in life, there is going to be a consequence whether it is good or bad. We all have to understand that we are not the only ones who are affected by the choices that we make. Yes, everybody makes mistakes, some people just happen to be in right place at the wrong time, and sometimes we do things out of desperation but we have to be more discerning and more aware of the things that we are doing and are exposed to. No one is immune from prison. The truth is that we are all just one bad choice away from ending up in prison. So we have to think and choose wisely. Our lives and the lives of the people that we love depend on it.

Chapter 10

Girl Talk 101

Since majority of our incarcerated loved ones are men, then ladies, I am going to speak directly to you. Now I understand that there are men that are going through the same situations as well, please feel free to use the gender interchangeably as it applies. So here goes. Let me start off by saying that I applaud all of you who chose to stand by your loved one during this difficult time. This life is in no way easy, at least not for those who truly stand ten toes down with their men. Between handling the everyday responsibilities that we come with our lives out here and maintaining a relationship with someone who is incarcerated, things can get pretty tough. We get stressed, agitated, frustrated, and irritated. Right now, the person that we love can't be with us. We love, miss, want, need, and desire them. We want them home and the fact that they can't be is just heartening. I understand that perfectly as I walk that same path with you.

During my relationship with Zulu, I have learned a lot of things. I have been through a lot with and for him. I have also come in contact with brothers who ask both my husband and I many questions about married life and just relationships in general that are as uniquely incredible as ours. Many see the type of relationship that my husband and I have and wonder how we make it work under these circumstances. The very first thing that I tell anyone is that our relationship is what we make of it. It is what we put into it. Not everyone is like my husband and not everyone is *like me. Everyone is different. People think and act differently. So the key is to be with someone that you are truly compatible with. It is to take the time to truly get to know a person before taking it to the next level. Time waits for no one but in this type of situation, time is all we have. Therefore, you have to utilize that to your advantage. You have to build a foundation. A house with a weak foundation will surely crumble.*

Now, I am by far a pro or expert when it comes to relationships. I am still learning and growing as well. However, I can only attest for what has worked for mine. Truth be told ladies, we can be our worst enemy. We can sabotage things and make things even greater than they have to be. And sometimes, it is justifiably so. Just because a man is incarcerated does not give them a free pass to do what the hell they want to do. In that same respect, just because he is incarcerated does not mean that we have the right to act like pure fools out here either. They are bounded by the same covenant that we are. But sometimes, we do take things to the extreme. Honestly, it is in our nature to be extreme. We are built on strength. We are built on emotion. We are filled with love. So yes, we can be extreme. We just have to understand what is really going on and understand the person that you are with. Again, it is all about growing and developing.

Our situation is uniquely incredible. The physical separation can be tough at times. I get that. Hell, I live, now 8-hours away from my husband. And even with being that far away, I can only see him twice a week in person. However, in between that time, we spend the rest of the time working on us and preparing for our future. Every day

*that you are blessed to wake up is a chance to learn
something different. It is a chance to live and do better than
you did the day before. It is a chance to be with the person
you love and explore the very essence of them. It is a chance
to live and love. However, during that learning process,
there will be times that you are tested. I have been through
that myself. So, because I have, let me share what I have
learned. Let's have some Girl Talk.*

*Point #1: Say what you mean and mean what you
say. See, in any situation, your word is your bond. Whatever
you say, it has to be stamped and sealed. When you are
with a man that is incarcerated, your word becomes 10
times powerful because that is all that they have to depend
on. They stand in faith on your word and trust that
whatever you say, that is what it is going to be. They are in
a place surrounded by uncertainty and unpredictability.
Things change up so much and they have to adapt to that
change at the drop of a hat. So they look for that honesty,
consistency and stability in the person that they love. Do
not sugar coat anything. If you can't do something, say
that. Don't have someone chasing a rainbow. Be upfront
and honest. So if you say something, mean it. Stick to your
guns.*

*Point #2: Loyalty is a must. Understand that loyalty
is more than just writing a letter, answering a call, or
coming to a visit. It is way more to it than that. Loyalty has
to do with faithfulness, allegiance, trustworthiness,
dependability, and reliability. All of those things are tied
into loyalty. Truth be told, men want a woman that they
can depend and trust just the same as a woman does. They
want a woman that is going to be there for them through it*

121

all, the good, bad, and the ugly. It is so easy for someone to be down and devoted when things are good. But what really counts is when you are able to stand by them and hold down the fort when things are not so good. So always be loyal.

Point #3: Be honest in your ways and actions. Conduct yourself as if he was standing on the outside of those walls. No double dipping. Now I am not saying that you can't go out, live, enjoy yourself, and have a good time. But just because your better half is incarcerated does not give you the green light to go and act a damn fool. You can't be in a relationship but conduct yourself as if you are single. You can't indulge in "single" activities when you are in a committed relationship. You can't live the double life. You can't be on the outside saying "Free My Baby" and slobbing him down on visitation day and then turning around giving it up like government cheese on the other days of the week. There is nothing worse than having the person that you love lose trust and respect for you, especially when it is just so simple to be open and honest. Now we all know that the truth may not always be pleasant to hear. But trust me; a person will respect you more if you are upfront and honest rather than the opposite. So, put it all on the table. If you are going to be friends, let the other know. If you are going to be committed to one another, make sure that is clear and set those boundaries. Blurred boundaries lead to misunderstandings and can just create a firestorm of unnecessary drama. Save yourself and the person you love the drama by just laying it all on the table.

Point #4: Be his peace. In a place filled with chaos and turmoil, a person looks to the one they love on the outside to provide comfort and encouragement. They look to us for that peace and sense of normalcy. Give him the opportunity to just relax, vent, and just absorb himself into you. Free his mind and spirit and allow him to mentally journey with you beyond the confines of the prison walls. Try not to complicate his day by the constant nagging and complaining about small superficial things. Often times, I have seen when women sit and complain when their sweetheart does not call at a particular time or complain when he is a little quiet and subdued. Prison is not predictable. Things change so frequently and suddenly. Remember, they are fighting a constant battle. They are amidst a struggle that some of us are unable to truly comprehend or understand. They will have bad days just like the rest of us. Now I am not saying not to address issues or tackle problems, but do it when the atmosphere between the two of you is calm and conducive to relaxed and peaceful conversation. Don't create another battlefield when he is already at war. Allow them the chance to retreat to that happy place that dwells inside of you and let them just stay for a little while.

Point #5: Take the time to really get to know the person that you are involved with. Before even considering marriage or a committed relationship, take the time to get to know someone first. See, most people subconsciously creatures of habit. And while they may be good at masking some things, eventually the truth will always come to surface. Time really does reveal. Pay close attention and listen to everything. Don't just listen to respond but really pay attention. Your intuition will never steer you wrong. If you start noticing red flags then that would be the time to address it and make the appropriate choice in accordance with your life and the goals that you have for yourself.

In a situation as unique as this, there are people who are only looking for a gain of some sort. From his perspective, it could be conversation and commissary or from her standpoint, it could be an ego booster, a means to control something, or a soothing to a bruised soul. But you have to take the time to really get to know a person. Right now, time is all you have so why not spend that getting to truly know a person. Once you truly get to know a person, you will be able to determine if what they are feeling is genuine or just some sort of game to play. A relationship is like an investment in your life. Take the time to really get to know someone and look out for your greatest asset, your heart.

Point #6: Be humble and grateful. I am blessed to know that my husband has a release date. There is a date that is set that will determine when this portion of the journey is over. However, I am not lost on the fact that there are people whose loved ones either have no release date, have dates that are extremely far away, or are not certain as to when their loved one will be released. And for those with the extended sentences, I love you and pray that you find the strength and peace to endure this all. As blessed as I am to know when my hubby returns, I am also not lost on the fact that things can happen. Circumstances change each and every day and situations arise. All it would take is one bad choice or one incident for that date to change. So I am always humble because I know that anything can happen. My blessing could easily turn into a bruising. It is natural to be happy and proud of the *accomplishments that our loved ones make from behind those walls, but be careful with how you approach that subject with others that share in the same struggle as you do. There is a difference between being happy and proud and boasting and bragging. The latter can be very hurtful and cause a lot of unnecessary pain and even resentment.*

Point #7: Watch what you post. We live in the new generation of social media. With that, people expose so much of their lives and the lives of their families to the general public. Social media has become a place where people come for so many reasons, from fun and games to fighting and feuding. There is nothing wrong with celebrating your love and your loved ones but remember to be mindful about the things that you post. Our loved ones are in prison and we have to remember that their thoughts, feeling, and desires matter as well. Refrain from talking about cases, posting unauthorized pictures, and deep personal things. Social media is public and no matter how many filters or privacy settings that you set, information can always have a way of being leaked and can have the potential to do more harm than good. So protect yourself and the one you love by limiting the content of your posts. Not everything is meant for everybody.

Point #8: Understand that these men have feelings too. Although they are in prison, that does not void the fact that they have real feelings and emotions. Not everyone behind the wall is a hardened, insensitive criminal. These men want and need to be loved, trusted, cherished, and respected just like the rest of us. Let me say this. Men finds true love, he becomes ten times the man that he was before, for he will truly know his purpose. Our incarcerated loved ones are in a place where they are dehumanized and institutionalized, and devoid from the personal contact of the outside world. A lot of them need love, want love, and are willing to give that love in return. Never take that for granted and play on their intelligences and emotions. I have met some of the most genuine, loving people behind the walls who have been simply dealt a bad hand and were forced to make some awful choices as a means of survival. I have met people who have never had or experienced real love from family members and others and just want someone to save them from the misery of their broken spirits. Protect their hearts just as you would protect yours. Be selfless and loving. Not everyone is going to hurt you or use you. While it is natural to be cautions, always remember to be kind. You would be surprised how something as simple as a letter, card, or even a smile could touch and lighten and heal the scar of a fragile heart.

Point #9: Take him out, not bring yourself in. I have noticed that some of us on the outside have gotten so engulfed in the politics of prison. There are people out here who know more about what goes on in there than the people that are in there do. They want to know who is doing what, who has what, and who is doing what with whom. To be honest, that is none of your business. If you want to concern yourself with something, make sure it is a worthy cause. Adequate treatment, access to healthcare, clean and safe conditions, and fair treatment are things that are worthy to be concerned with. The entire he said, she said, I saw, they did, he got stuff is just irrelevant and brings more problems than solutions. Most men don't want to sit and talk about all that. They don't want to be *reminded and constantly discussing what goes on in a place that they desperately want to get out of. You can't take him away physically but you sure can bring his mind out of that place and let me take in some of you. And in this case, some instances of ignorance truly is bliss. Sometimes, the less you know the better.*

Point #10: Don't forget about you. It is so easy to get wrapped up in making sure that our loved ones behind the wall are ok. As a woman, it is in our nature to want to make sure that those we love are safe, healthy, and comfortable. You want to take every phone call, make every visit, and write 5 letters a week. But life still goes on out here and those things can get a little taxing on us. Take the time to take care of yourself. You are not a robot or a machine. You can only do the best that you can. And even still, you must take that time and look after yourself. You still have to live. Having a life of your does not mean that you don't love his. It simply means that you have to care for yourself just as much as you care for him. Take that time to go shopping for that cute pair of shoes, or take that class that you have wanted to take, or go out for that girl's night out, or go have that spa date and have that manicure and pedicure that you so desperately need. Have some outside interest that you enjoy doing and focus on making yourself into an even greater woman than you are now. There is no shame or blame in that. It is so easy to get burned out from all of this. The last thing that you want to do is get so bothered and stressed that you start snapping at your loved one. That will cause problems and breakdown your relationship. Remember, you can only do but so much. You can only make him feel as good as you do. Energy feeds off one another. If you are in a good head space then you can pass that positivity onto him and together both of you will radiate as bright as the sun.

Point #11: Learn to truly love yourself. Until you learn how to truly love yourself, you will poison all of your relationships by allowing the scars of the past to resurface in the present. I will admit, being with someone in prison can meet you with a little apprehension but allow that apprehension to be based on things that you see in front of you. Do not bring in baggage from old relationships. It is not the job of your loved one to heal you. That is something that you have to do for yourself. That is something that is for God and you to take care of. Love without fear. Live without excess baggage. Have you ever stopped to wonder why a rearview mirror of a car is so small but the windshield is so wide. I like to think that it is because the past is behind you and as you move away from it, the things that were behind you become smaller and then disappear. But the windshield is in front of you. It is big, so that you can see the wide view through your journey and to your destination. Your future is yours for the taking. Don't spend precious time living a moment that you have already lived. Embrace yourself, love yourself, and accept yourself, flaws and all. Once you truly love yourself, then loving someone else will come so easily.

Now I know that I have not said everything that there is to say in just these few pointers, and as my own personal disclaimer, I do not claim to know everything about every situation and every relationship. I can only attest to what I know from my own personal experience. These things are not something that I read in a book or saw on a television show. All of these things come from my own life and my personal experience in being in a relationship with a person that is incarcerated.

Chapter 11

Guy Talk 101

Since I just had my little talk with the ladies, now it's time for me to have my little few moments with the guys. Guys, let me start off by saying that I salute you all. It takes a lot to be able to endure all that you do and still try to stay focused on the future and making better choices in life. It is my hope that you take this time and really prepare yourself for the wonderful things that await you in life. It is my prayer that you take this time and reflect on the actions of your past and that you use those things to restructure and reshape your future. Prison is just your location. It does not define who you are. You do.

Point #1: Be upfront and honest in your ways and in your actions. Truth be told, women will walk through fire and hell with you if they believe and trust in you. Trust is so easy to get but it is hard as hell to get back once it is broken. Be righteous in your ways and actions. Men are natural born leaders. If you want a woman to follow your lead, you have to be walking the path of righteousness yourself. Say what you mean and mean what you say. Remember that we are stepping out on faith and believing in you in a world that tells us not to. We are looking past your convictions and misfortunes and wanting to love you for who you truly are. We want from you the same things that you want from us. Your word is your bond and we hold you to that. We hold you accountable for the things that you do just as you should do with us. You can only give as good as you get. So always make your intentions clear and make your word stand for something more than just a cute little speech.

Point #2: You are bounded by the same rules as the women. What that simply means is that you can't have your cake and eat it too. Just because you are incarcerated does not give you a free pass to act like a complete damn fool either. When or if you agree to a relationship while you are incarcerated, you have to conduct yourself in the same manner that you would if you were out here in the free world. You don't get to have multiple women coming to visit or writing love letter to both her and Suzy. You can't expect to be treated like a king and then treat the other person like a piece of trash. You don't get side pieces or hoes. Respect is everything. When you are in a relationship, it is your responsibility to make the other person feel comfortable, happy, and full of joy. Now I am not saying that it is your job to cure a nagger. But it is your job to not give her a reason to nag. Be her comforter, her peace, and shower with all the love that you have.

Point #4: Be appreciative of her efforts. Visits, phone calls, letters, and commissary take on a whole world of its own. Yes, we know how important these things are to you and you look forward to these things. Understand that we know what it takes to make you feel comfortable and to build and nurture our relationships. But please understand that although you have to be there, we have to be here. And with that, there is the responsibility of bills, food, car notes, kids, and shelter. There may be a time when she is not able to come up for a visit or send money for commissary. She may not be able to write you 5 days a week, maybe only 2 days a week because she is working or going to school.

Don't make her feel bad about that, especially if there is a valid reason for it. Now if she is sitting at home, doing nothing, then you have every reason to feel a kind of way. But is she is out here working and all cut her a break. We are aware that you are fighting a battle that few people truly know about or even care to understand. I have seen enough videos and documentaries to know that prison is not the place that you want to be. But understand that the things that we do are because we love you and want you to be ok while you are there. We do those things because we care.

Point#5: There is a such thing as loyalty. So many guys that I have run across in prison often say that there is no loyalty. Not every woman that you meet is out here to hurt you or play with your feelings. Not every woman is trying to control or manipulate you. There are women out here that truly love and care for you. There are women who are looking for the same love and affection as you. Yes, you do run across some people with ulterior motives. But you have to take the time to get to know someone. Time will reveal a person's true intentions and trust me, whatever is done in the dark will certainly some to the light. Trust your instincts. When a person shows you who they really are, believe them.

Understand, that you have the right to be happy as well and have someone by your side that is going to conduct themselves properly. They don't get a free pass to hurt you either just because you are incarcerated. Just think about it like this. You are in one of the gloomiest places in the world. If a woman gets involved with you and can make those gloomy day a little sunnier, then she is a keeper. If she is true, genuine, and loyal to you in her ways and actions, then she is a keeper. If you feel as if you can trust her completely, then she is a keeper. Be loyal to her as she is to you.

Point #6: Make your life count. We all understand that you are in there for a reason. But as I said before, prison is just a location. It does not define who you are. Do the time, don't let it do you. Get into the books, study, and work hard. Physically you are behind the wall but your mind is not limited to anything. Prepare and strengthen yourself emotionally and spiritually. Elevate yourself, you're your purpose, and rise to the occasion. Look in the mirror every day and tell yourself that you are going to be a better man than you were the day before. Be a leader, someone that you can others can talk to and learn from. Read, study, focus, and build yourself to be stronger than you were when you first arrived.

Just because prisons are lacking in rehabilitation efforts, don't allow that to interfere with self-motivation and self- knowledge. History constantly refers to men that have educated and learned things on their own. Have a plan. Don't just sit back and surround yourself with all of the crap that goes on in prison. Yes, you are around it. But being around it and being in it are two different things. Know and learn the difference.

Point #7: Your actions do not only affect you. Please understand that when something happens to you and with you, it is not only you that is affected. People that love and care for you bear the same amount of anger, worry, confusion, aggravation, and frustration as you do. If you were to get into something and have to go to the hole, imagine how that would feel to the ones that you leave out here. It is already unpleasant enough with just you being in there. But if you couple that with even more limitations and restrictions, imagine how difficult that would be. Just think if someone got used to hugging you and kissing you every weekend for months and then all of a sudden, you are restricted to only seeing them through glass and only for a short amount of time. How would you feel? How do you think that person would feel? Now I understand that things happen and a lot of things you can't control. However you can control yourself. Think before you act because your thoughts not only govern your actions but also the outcome.

Point #8: Listen and balance. Understand that sometimes we don't want you to fix our problems. We want you to just listen. We want you to listen to how it's cold outside or how our co-worker stole our parking spot or that the kids want pizza instead of chicken for dinner. We want you to assure us that tomorrow is going to be better and that today was just a rough one. We want you to just soothe our spirits with your loving voices and you incredible understanding. But we also want you to listen to when a problem arises or something in the relationship is not going right. We want you to listen to how we feel and not disregard our feelings and thoughts simply because you don't understand them. We want you to balance. Balance your time playing cards with the guys or playing ball on the court with some conversation and attention to us. Understand that we require your time, love, and attention also.

Point #9: You have the right to be loved. Just because you are behind the wall does not mean that you are not loved or that you have the right to be mistreated. I tell people all the time, "Do not awaken feelings in someone if you do not intend on loving really loving them". No one wants to be hurt; no one wants a broken heart. I don't know a person in the world who got pleasure out of being used or discarded. There are people out here who want the best for you, want a life with you, and want to love you. The key is to be receptive to that. Your lives matter to so many people. It is possible for you to find love behind the wall. However, in order for you to receive that love from behind the wall, you have to tear the wall down from around your heart. Love is a beautiful thing when it is pure and unconditional.

Point #10: We want to matter to you. Relationships are a two-way street. You get out of it what you put into it. This situation is unique and there are limitations to the physical things that you can do. But this is the perfect time to make love to each other's minds and shower one another with all the love and affection that is possible. We want and need to love you and you want that same reciprocation. With the right person, this is a time to create, build, and nurture a budding and promising relationship that can grow into something even more beautiful and more meaningful. Love yourself and love the person that loves you wholeheartedly and unconditionally. Do that not out of fear or desperation but for the mere fact that this person is the one for you.

Guys, understand this, I know that the aspect of having a relationship in prison can give you a little cause for hesitation. But as my husband can attest, if you meet the right one and work to create this sacred bond, then it will definitely bring you such joy, peace, and happiness and that is something that no guard or no amount of time can take away from you.

Chapter 12

Look, listen, and be heard

Ignorance is not always bliss. We are living in a time where being knowledgeable and informed is a must. In many cases, it is even as important as life and death. We all have access to televisions, radio, and social media. So we can easily have access to information and current events that are happening around us. Because these matters affect us and our loved ones, we must listen and pay attention to what is happening around us.

I can't begin to tell you about the numerous atrocities and misfortunes that I have read about in regards to our prison system. There are many people who have been injured, wrongfully accused, mistreated, misdiagnosed, abused, and even killed within the walls of the prison. With my husband being in that same situation, I worry about his safety and well-being all the time. I know that he can take care of himself but when there are forces that are greater than you with more access to resources that you don't have, you are put in a serious disadvantage. Now I know and understand that prison is not designed to be a place of luxury or convenience, but I do feel that all people should be treated fairly, respectfully, and humanely. There should never be a time when asking a simple question could cost you your life.

You wouldn't believe how many stories I have read about inmates being physically, mentally, and sexually assaulted by offices who took an oath to protect. It is hard to fathom at the foods that they are being fed and the limited or either no access to healthcare and basic necessities. Yes, that "three hots in a cot" cliché may seem to be enough but it goes further than that. Sometimes those hots are cold and those cots are bare. Nevertheless, they are forced to deal with those issues. Prison is like a complete world of its own. They govern themselves and make up their own rules and regulations as they see fit. And if there are things that happen behind the wall, it is usually kept quiet until it gets bigger than what they can handle.

Let me say this. Pay attention and listen to the things that your loved ones say. Watch them closely and look for changes that occur within them. Monitor their attitudes and mannerisms as much as you can. This can give you clues to how they live and the stuff that they have to endure on the inside. Look for changes in their physical appearance as well. Ask questions and clarification on marks that cannot be explained. If at any time, you feel as if something is going wrong or their safety, well-being, or lives are in jeopardy, call and ask questions. Familiarize yourself with important phone numbers and addresses to the prison officials and administration. Go the distance, make calls, send emails, and voice your concerns. Be their voices and let their cares and concerns be heard. It is too important not to. Always advocate for your loved one.

During the course of my relationship, I have had numerous interactions and encounters with prison administration and officials. I have voiced my concerns in regards to issues dealing with my husband. My main concerns have been with his fair treatment and his education. Now I will admit, some of the staff are attentive and look to resolve issues. However, there are others who look at my calling and inquiring as a jab at them and seek to do nothing but get me off the phone. There are even times when I have felt like my husband was targeted by staff simply because I have questioned and challenged their "authority". It was more of a deterrent to keep me from going above their heads or even getting my person legal team involved. And yes, it has been that serious. I cannot say that this could not and would not happen to you but the mere fact that my concerns have been heard and documented puts them on notice that I will not just lay back and allow my husband to be mistreated or dehumanized simply because he is a prisoner. He has rights as well and I am going to see that he is able to exercise those that he is lawfully entitled to.

I have met some incredible people who all share that same passion and devotion to those they love. I have shied away from "prison wife" groups, simply because they are not of my taste. There may be some great ones out there and by all means, if that is your cup of tea, then join for some support. The ones that I have encountered have been nothing more than a circus full of hating, gossip, drama, and cattiness. And that is just something that I do not have any time or tolerance for. However, I have conversed with founders and members of advocacy groups and have even networked with others who genuinely share in the same sentiment of protecting and seeking fair treatment of our incarcerated loved ones. Their stories are inspiring and bring to light issues that would either go unnoticed or ignored.

Being heard is more than just calling and cursing people out about some missing socks or no cable on the *television. It is not just about mediocre things. Advocacy is about tackling and speaking up on issues that involve the preservation of life, heath, liberties, and safety. The prison system in general needs to undergo some serious restructuring and revitalization. Corporate greed, politics, and the need for power have created a system that is designed to keep our loved ones at a disadvantage. These issues have created a breeding ground for chaos, despair, and deprivation under the umbrella of rehabilitation. It just seems that more punishment is going on rather than rehabilitation. Our men and women are being locked up at an alarming rate for longer periods of time. Those who are fortunate to be released are often placed back into society without having acquired the skills and resources needed to live in society. Because of that lack, they revert back to what they know, creating a revolving door and increasing their chances of recidivism. Prison systems are paid by tax dollars to governments and corporate entities that profit from our loved ones being incarcerated. We can safely say that something needs to be done.*

Just as our loved ones are there to be held accountable for their wrongs, prison officials need to be held accountable as well. In your spare time, search on the internet and you will find countless individuals who have found themselves on the other side of the fence due to their own negligent and despicable behaviors. These are the same people that took an oath to uphold laws and abide by certain standards that were in positions of authority to which our loved ones had to answer to. The bottom line is that these officials are paid by our tax dollars. Because of that, we have the right to ask questions and seek answers to the issues of our loved ones. You should be free to do that without retaliation or retribution to yourself or your loved one. We have the right to know that our loved ones are being corrected in an environment that is free from abuse, neglect, and cruel or unusual punishment. They have the right to an education and to obtain resources and services needed to increase their chances of success upon their release.

There are a few prison systems that have forums, meet and greets, and town hall type meetings that allow the families of prisoners to come in and talk and discuss issues. Whenever you can, attend them. It is there that you can find out a wealth of information and meet with prison officials to discuss concerns and get answers to questions. But do not let that be the only time that you speak up. Place a face with those state numbers and let them know that although they are prisoners, they are loved by others and have support out here in the free world. Don't just let anything happen, hear and be heard. We have to be the listeners and voices for our loved ones that are behind the wall.

Chapter 13

After all is said and done

Being the wife of a prisoner is not an easy one. It takes a lot of love, time, devotion, and patience to be able to deal with everything that comes with maintaining and sustaining a relation with someone who is in prison. It is not always easy but then and again, nothing in life worth having is easy. There have been tears, fears, insecurities, confusion, misunderstandings and uncertainties. But that has also been joy, happiness, peace, comfort, understanding, and love. My husband and I have a marriage that is strong and built on a foundation of love, trust, respect, and devotion. There are times when we are not necessarily pleasant to one another and we say or do things that do not honor the vows that we have taken. We have made mistakes and been foolish with one another but at the end of the day, we are married and we are determined to make it work. We rely on one another and our faith to pull us through whatever trial or tribulation that we may face. We relish our triumphs and successes in unison as well.

I am always inspired by a quote from an unknown author that simply says, "You never know how strong you are until being strong is the only choice that you have." This resonates with me so well because I am a strong and independent woman. I chose to love this man, in this situation, with the understanding that this was not going to be just a walk in the park. I decided to marry this man knowing that we would have hurdles to climb and struggles *that we would have to overcome. I look to no one but God, my husband, and myself to sustain me. It takes loyalty and strength to deal with a situation such as mine. It takes character to look past the flaws and imperfections of a person and love them despite of the things that they have done. So often, we judge others without taking the time to understand or even entertain the notion that people have the right to live their lives in a way that is conducive to them. As long as they are not causing hurt, harm, or danger to anyone, then what business is it as to how they live their lives? People also tend to think that a person is not capable of change or a chance at redemption. I believe that chance should be given to anyone who truly seeks to obtain it.*

Strength comes from within. We have to learn that we cannot look to people to fix the things that are emotionally bothersome to us and it is not their jobs. It is something that we have to fix ourselves. It is then and only then that we will be give and receive the love that we require. We have to build the strength from inside, hold on tight to it, and apply it through our daily walk throughout life. We have all experienced things that were not pleasing and in some cases, those things were very painful. But it's those things that will either make us or break us. Each chapter in my life has taught me more about myself and allowed me to grow into the type of woman that I can be proud of. Each lesson learned, some extremely hurtful as taught me about my level of endurance and my tenacity and my will to achieve greatness in everything that I set out to do. When you have proven your strength to yourself, you have achieved an elevated sense of courage that is yours and yours alone. When you come up against fear and anxiety, you have rally against it. You hold on to that faith and your inner strength and press forward.

Being in prison is hard. It's tough on everyone, not just the prisoner. For every day that a person has to give, it's a day that is taken from someone else. It's a moment of preciousness that cannot be given back. There days when you are floating on cloud nine and days when you are sad, but that is life. It's not going to be peaches and cream everyday but if you learn to take the bitter with the sweet, then everything will work out. It is easy to love and be dedicated when things are going good but what matters is your ability to love and remain loyal when things are not going so good. That is when you will truly know how strong your relationship is. A true testament to a relationship is when you can conquer all the things that were set up to destroy it.

Whenever I think of Zulu, I think of so many things. I think of his incredible heart, his ability to lead, his willingness and determination to come out of this situation better than he did when he went in. When I think of him, I think of strength, joy, and peace. When I think of him, I think of his stubbornness, his arrogance, his ability to sometimes make me feel like biting nails, and I think of the way his voice sounds when he calls me "spoiled". When I think of him, I think of his wisdom, his passion, his devotion, his laughter. Even with all that I think of, the most incredible of all is love. It's the definition of love that I get from the Bible. Love truly is patient and love truly is kind. That is the way that it is supposed to be. Love is not created out of fear or desperation, it is created out of the beautiful medley of feelings that you have for another person. It's the *feeling of devotion and understanding, of loyalty and honesty, of faith and perseverance. We have laid a foundation built on our faith in God and each other and with a combination like that, we can't lose. We are a team and we stand hand in hand together and against anything that threatens to harm or separate us, growing together mentally and spiritually. While we are not lost on the fact that marriage of any kind takes a lot of hard work, we are both committed to making this work.*

My goal is to defeat the odds that say that couples who are married to someone who is in prison will end in divorce. That is not just because I want to prove the statistics and other people wrong. It is because I want to prove to myself and to my husband that what we are strong enough to handle anything that comes our way. We do not stand on the jaded ideologies and tainted opinions of others. We see our life through our eyes and we rely solely on God and each other to sustain us. The foundation that we have built is ours and only we can destroy it or allow it to be destroyed. If our love and perseverance can get us through this, then we can get through anything. Love and loyalty is incredible and that is exactly what we have.

Granted, I may fuss a little more, push him a little harder, and demand more out of him but it is because I know who he is, what he has the potential to become, and that there is no one rooting more for his success than I am. This man is my better half. I am a Queen and he is my King and together, we will walk down that path of righteousness, focused and undeterred. His successes and failures are mine, as mine are his. Our triumphs and tribulations are shared. I know what his life is worth to me and I want him to live up to and be everything that he is destined to be. There is so much more to him than a stripes and a prison identification number. With everything that we have both been through, we owe it to ourselves to live abundantly and peacefully. As his wife, I want the chance to experience the life that we were destined to live that extends greater and far beyond razor-wired fences and correctional officers.

There are some people who will never understand why I have made the choice to marry and stand by my husband while he is in prison. They want to know what it is that he can do for me or what is it that he wants, and all other kinds of cynical questions. I am not going to sit and decipher the motives for line of questioning but I will answer their questions using one general statement and that is "I know that this was a personal choice of mine, one which I made solely based on love and commitment to the man that I feel was created just for me. I did not make this decision based on anything other than that. There is no fear, desperation, foolishness, or stupidity involved on my part.

I am fully aware of everything that I must endure and every possibility coming into this marriage. I am secure and comfortable enough in myself to know that being his wife is not just who I am but who I was destined to be". Yes, you may face all kinds of opposition and mean-spirited opinions from all kinds of people who are irrelevant to your relationship. But if you are secure in what you have and what you want, then you are not going to be the least bit interested in what the next person will say or how they may feel. This is because at the end of the day, none of that is going to matter. I am not in a relationship with them, I am with him.

Now I am not saying that this is an ideal situation. No one wakes up in the morning and say "hey, I want to marry someone in prison". I don't know of anyone who would choose this type of relationship on purpose. It would have to be for a purpose other than just having someone to call your own, maybe even something dealing with some physiological issue or deep-seated need. There would really have to be something greater in order to go through a relationship that can be so complexed and consuming. My relationship is something that happened ordinarily under an extraordinary circumstance. Now I am not endorsing or promoting prison marriage, I am just merely talking about me and my personal choice to marry the man that I love who just happens to be incarcerated. Although some people may not understand my choice, it is a choice that I have made and one that I stand completely and wholeheartedly.

Marriage is about so much more than just the wedding day and the vows. In fact, that is the simplest day of marriage. What happens the rest of the days is what counts. I have come to accept the fact that every day is not going to be sunny days and candlelight. There are going to be days when things are not going to be right. You wake up feeling bad and you lay in bed alone and then you wonder why you decided to do this. Sometimes, you feel like you want to just give up and throw in the towel. You get up and start your day with no morning kiss or breakfast in bed and it is sitting at the breakfast table when the sound of silence speaks louder than ever. Your heart begins to ache and tears start to fill the wells of your eyes. Just when that one tear is about to fall, the phone rings and it is the voice of the person that you are missing on the other end. Suddenly you forget about the first waking hour and you are reminded as to why you love this person so much. You think about the gift of the day that God blessed you with and you get up and move forward, making every precious moment count.

Married life has been an adventure, full of twists and turns. There are some days when I feel like I am floating on cloud nine and then there are other days when I feel like pulling my hair out. There are some days when I love him to pieces and other days when I want to just shake the hell out of him. But even after all of that, I know that he is the person that I want to spend the rest of my life with. Just as with any married couple, we experience problems but what we have is compromise, loyalty, respect, understanding, trust, devotion, and of course love. These things are essential for a healthy marriage. It not just about going through something but growing through it. As long as we hold onto our faith, remain consistent in our prayer, trust, apologize, forgive, understand, and honor the vows that we have taken then we can and will beat the odds that are stacked against us.

One of the most incredible lessons that I have learned is that love is love. When you love someone there is no controlling that. It is supposed to be unconditional. You are not supposed to control who you love. The love that I have for my husband is beautiful and sacred. It is something wonderful, beautiful, and exclusively reserved for him and him alone. The space that he occupies in my heart is shared by no man other than God. The amount of

*loyalty and devotion that I have for him surpasses
anything. I have always wanted him to have the things that
he needs and I support him wholeheartedly on every
decision that he has made. Yes, I may have an opinion
about it and I may even fuss about it, but I love him enough
to share and support his visions even when he thinks that I
don't understand. It is so easy to get wrapped up in prison
life and all of the negative connotations that are associated
with it. However, when you really take the time to past that
in delve deeper into that person, you see something that is
so beautiful. After all the searching, the scrutiny, and
everything that you have to go through, there is never a
more incredible moment than to be able to sit and stare in
the eyes of the person that you love so very much, the
person that completes you.*

*When I see Zulu, I do not see the uniform, the walls,
the bars, or the officers. All I see is the man that I love and
who loves me. I see the person that sees all of my flaws,
failures, and imperfections and loves me despite of them. I
see a person who shows me the meaning of real love, who
teaches me, who expands my mind to the limitless
possibilities. I see a person who challenges my archaic ways
of thinking and shows me to open my mind and believe in
the impossible. I have a husband who fosters my growth,
nurtures my thoughts, and supports my vision. Loving him
makes me a better me, as he will happily attest that I have
done the same for him. It is not out of desperation,
apprehension, or desolation but out of a pure love and the
desire to live a life of happiness. I think that is something
that everyone wants. Everyone dreams of having someone
to share their lives with. Those dreams are not limited to*

people that are in the free world. Those cares and those hopes extend far, wide, and beyond the prison walls. While some people still will never understand, it is my life. I love my husband completely and wholeheartedly and there is no shame or no blame in that. I make no apologies for the choice that I have made.

All in all, it has been an incredible journey. It is full of twist and turns, full of love and joy, full of trials and tribulations. While prison is a dark and dreary place, it is a place where those who seek it can find peace, redemption, and correction. It is place where you can learn, grow, and develop into a shadow of your former self and emerge into a life of joy, peace, and love. In my case, it is a place where I found true love, where the better half of my heart temporarily dwells. Although this is not the life that I chose, my path in life is was predestined and I now must play the hand that I was dealt. Prison is designed to hold you physically, to cut you off from the rest of the world. But your mind, heart, and spirit are free to roam, seek, and find. I am living proof that although the prison may hold his physical self, his mental, spiritual, and emotional being dwells within mine. There is no distance that is far enough or no fence that is wide enough to keep me from him. My heart and spirit are filled with an abiding and sacred love that belongs to him and only him. Some may inquire and some may wonder, but at least now, you know what life is like inside the walls of my Incarcerated Heart.

My Love Letter to My Husband

I wish that there was another word besides "love" that I could say that would completely describe what feel for you. I tell you that I love you every day and for some reason that word just does not seem sufficient enough. What I feel for you is sweeter than any peach, softer than any cotton, and stronger than any piece of steel. What I feel for you is closer than any distance, is not separated by any fence, and is unbounded by any letter. It is not scrutinized by any guard or locked behind any doors. What I feel for you is unconditional and without boundaries. What I have inside me sees you for the incredible man that you are, imperfectly perfect for me. It fills me with joy and pride to know that I was your first choice, the woman that you chose. You saw me for who I was, flaws and all and yet you still chose me. You solidified your commitment to me by making me your wife, as I now carry your last name. It makes my heart skip a beat when I say your name. I am left breathless from the way you draw me closer into you by the taste of your soft lips. What I feel for you gives me strength that I never knew I had. It ignites a fire in me to fight when I feel like giving up. It brings me peace when I am surrounded by turmoil and drama. What I feel for you comforts me, dries my tears, and erases my fears. It takes away all doubts and uncertainties. What I feel allows me to relax completely in your arms, casting away all sounds in the room except for the rhythm of your heart which beats perfectly in sync with mine. What I feel for you allows me to give of myself freely unto you, in my mind, body, and spirit.

It allows me to be loyal, truthful, and respectful in my ways and actions. What I feel for you makes me a better me. Like I said, I wish there was a bigger, more incredible word to truly describe how I really feel. However, the only word besides "love" that comes to my mind is my "Zulu". And it dawned on me that the best way to describe these beautiful things is to know the reason that I feel all of them. My darling, that reason is you; my love, my life, my Zulu. Always Remember, Never Forget...Forever You, Forever Me, Forever We....

Love Always,

Your Wife,

Shelle

I lovingly dedicate this book to my great-grandfather, the late Lacy Crenshaw. He was the first person to ever put a piece of paper in front of me and a pencil in my hand. He saw something great in me a long time ago and he knew that one day, I was going to make that piece of paper and pencil speak. I love you, Granddaddy. I hope I have made you proud.

To my father-in-law, the late, Willie Everette Hooper, my Superman, I thank you for always showing me unconditional love and respect. Your integrity and honesty is something that I will always cherish. Thank you for welcoming me with open arms not just into your family but in your heart. You have always been there for us, always guiding us. Your faith in our marriage and us as individuals is incredible. Continue to watch over us. I love you and miss you terribly.

To my aunt, Vernell, I thank you for always standing in my corner and always being supportive throughout my entire life. You have always encouraged and fostered my dreams. I love you so much and I thank you for your unconditional love and support.

To my mother, Adriane, I love you more than you can ever know. I owe everything that I am to you. Thank you for teaching me about life, love, and never losing sight of my goals and dreams. I appreciate all of your love, advice, and support.

To my brothers and sisters who share in the same struggle, I love you all. Just know that I think of and pray for you often. May you all find the love, peace, and strength to travel this journey. I know that it is not easy and the load gets hard to carry but know that strength dwells within you and coupled with love, you can and will conquer anything. Know that you don't walk it alone, for I walk it proudly and boldly with you.

www.ingramcontent.com/pod-product-compliance
Lightning Source LLC
Chambersburg PA
CBHW050129280326
41933CB00010B/1309